All

The

Things

MARIAH MARTINEZ

Copyright © 2023 MARIAH MARTINEZ

All rights reserved.

ISBN: 9798872708926

This book is based on my personal experience and the information is not intended nor otherwise implied to be a substitute or replacement for medical advice, diagnosis, or treatment from a mental health or medical professional. No action or inaction should be taken based solely on the contents of this information. Always consult your physician or other qualified healthcare provider for your own situation. If you think you have a medical emergency, call your doctor or 911 immediately.

DEDICATION

I once heard a TED talk where a woman was describing how she wanted to thank herself more. She said that we, as women, never take credit for anything we do, yet our male counterparts don't think twice about it. So, I want to start by thanking myself, for not only thinking of the idea but putting my thoughts and words to paper and writing this book.

I want all the people who are thinking of becoming parents to know they are not alone. I want social support systems to have a little insight into what it feels like having children and how to support parents. I want people to know there is help out there and not only how to find it, but demand it.

To single moms who have to do it all by themselves; to my kids so they will be a little more prepared than I was if they choose to have kids; to those people who are changing the narrative in society and sharing what the true motherhood journey can look like:

This book is dedicated to you.

As Alicia Keys says in "Superwoman,"
"Cause I am a superwoman
Yes, I am, Yes, she is
See, even when I'm a mess
I still put on a vest
With an S. on my chest
Oh yes, I'm a superwoman."

We are all superwomen and cheers to us to waking up every day and being who we were meant to be.

CONTENTS

PREFACE

To the one who feels like they're losing themselves...

To the ones who act like they have it all together, but don't…

To the ones who look perfect on the outside, but on the inside feel like they're losing it all...

You are not alone.

Walk with me through my journey and know that I'm okay and it's okay not to be ok.

Once I had my two kids—currently six and three years old—friends, coworkers and acquaintances thinking about starting a family began asking me for any advice I might have.

From the trauma I've had in giving birth and postpartum, my instantaneous and blunt response was, "Don't do it yet."

After having my kids, I continued to have the thought, why didn't anyone tell me all the things I would need to know about having a baby? Why did my family only talk about all the joys of having kids? Poking, and prodding about when we would grow our family, yet never talked about postpartum or miscarriages?

Why do some doctors warn you, while others don't tell you anything about what you are able and not able to do during pregnancy, birthing or breast-feeding pain, complications, or the possibility of having a c-section? Let alone what even is a c-section. There are so many questions in my head that cause anger and frustration that people didn't talk about but should have.

So many of these subjects are taboo in modern society. But I feel they should be in the forefront of everyone's minds when thinking about having a baby. I don't understand why we would treat such a huge change in a person's life like a fun game of "Taboo." Tiptoeing around complicated subjects and making most of us guess our way through birthing and raising another human being. Talking about it out loud would ease that feeling of being alone once having kids. Knowing that other people are going through the same thing as you, that you are not crazy and that your feelings are valid, is a lifeline.

We grow up as little girls encouraged to think that this is the goal in life; fall in love, have a family, buy a house with a white picket fence, and absolutely love being a mom. Along with these external factors, we also have internal factors where we lower our own expectations of what we want to achieve in order to become another version of ourselves. Internally we tell ourselves that we can wait to achieve our own goals.
Is there even a more amazing goal than becoming a mother?

We shouldn't move out too early. We don't need to try different jobs to see what we like. We don't need to go to the out-of-state college. We don't need to travel yet. We don't need to explore what is out there. We shouldn't date around. We make ourselves shrink into who others think we should be, so that we don't rock the boat. Don't go against the grain. Don't make people have a reason to question or doubt you.

Especially being Hispanic—if we fail, our parents fail too.

I want to make sure women know that their life is not an audition to be somebody's wife or mother. This book will teach you how to make small adjustments to keep your identity as I share my own story of how I went from wanting kids, dreading having kids, and learning how to keep my own identity with kids.

After having kids, I knew I had to share my story in the hopes that it would help others avoid going down a narrow path, alone, in the dark. I lean on my personal experiences, and not only what I've learned through this process of becoming a "mom", but also, truly becoming me.

If this book helps just one person, it would be worth it for me. I am in no way trying to write a "self-help" or "guide" on how to have a baby because each journey is incredibly different and although I didn't have a great experience, others may have had worse, or even better experiences. And that's not what this book is about.

I also understand not everyone will be able to relate to this book. Some people may not want to have kids, some may want kids so bad but have a really hard time or are not able to have them, and some may feel like it's too late to change a choice they've previously made. All of these are things are valid and true but it's not my story. I hope that even if this may be you, that you would find some sort of hope in this book that may help even if it's just one thing.

Also, just to clarify, I am *not* saying that I don't love my kids, or I wish I'd never had them. They are one of the most important journeys in my life, and through therapy, I have learned to cherish the small moments, and be present with them before the time passes by too quickly. The moments when my daughter tells me, "I love you forever," in a squeaky little voice, or the giant hugs my son gives me with a kiss on the cheek, completely melt my heart.

The joy of having kids is like I'm riding a roller coaster with many ups and some downs but still freefalling into love. And as F.B.I. operative Gracie Hart (Sandra Bullock) famously said in *Miss Congeniality*, "If anyone, anyone tries to hurt them, I would take them out. I would make them suffer so much that they'd wish they were never born. And if they ran, I would hunt them down."

But even in loving my kids unconditionally, there was a lot of unexpected pain both physically and emotionally that I endured.

So please, share this with everyone you love who may be thinking about, or is in the early journey of, having kids. I hope that even those not thinking of having kids will be able to read this from their own perspective and apply some of the concepts in their personal or professional lives. I also hope that those who have people in their lives who are thinking about having kids, or have kids, know a little more about how to support them.

In the end, this is my journey to self-appreciation and self-awareness of one's goodness, and if I can throw in a few tips on how to keep your identity while having a baby, that's the best of both worlds.

Know that I'm not perfect. I'm not always happy and I don't "have it all." This marathon of life is only the beginning of my journey. I cannot wait to share all the information I've gained over the years. I don't know what the next step is in God's plan for my life, but I do know that I'm not in control of the big picture. And yet, I can be in control of small life-changing decisions. You set your own expectations. We get to do life, not how society defines us, but by defining our own way forward with the people supporting us. That is my definition of happiness.

" IT DOES GET BETTER, AND THERE ARE *Beautiful* MOMENTS WAITING FOR YOU. THERE ARE *Beautiful* PEOPLE WAITING TO LOVE YOU AND ONE OF THOSE PEOPLE IS YOURSELF."

~Pink

CHAPTER 1

The Fairytale

My rose-colored glasses shattered the moment the little pink lines appeared on the pregnancy test. A feeling of excitement, though also doom that my life was over, overwhelmed my soul. 

Since I was a little girl, I had waited for this moment. All I ever wanted was a good job that paid well, a nice house that had a perfect little white-picket fence with not a blade of grass out of order, a handsome husband who supported me, and two little kids (a boy and girl of course). If I had all that, my life would be complete. No ifs, ands, or buts about it. I'm not sure at what point in my life this became the goal, but I certainly remember feeling this as early as elementary school.

I also saw this dream represented on television. I used to watch Lucille Ball from *I Love Lucy*, (with my mom and grandma), roam around the house doing silly housework while the audience laughed hysterically when she made something look or sound funny. I watched Selena striving to make a career out of singing, but not being able to find herself because she couldn't be with the *one,* she loved, or start a family because of her singing career.

I used to watch my mom love being a mom. I remember being a child and wanting to give my kids the same fun and joyful childhood I had. I don't ever remember my mom saying it was hard, she was tired, or needed a break. That's not saying she wasn't exhausted or didn't want to do it anymore because now I get it. You may be at your wits end, but you may also be sitting on the floor, playing tea party pretending like there's nowhere else you'd rather be smiling through anything.

I remember early in my childhood going to work with my mom after school. I would see her being the manager of people, behind a big wooden desk, with a huge rolodex of numbers thinking, *wow she's so powerful in charge and has it all.* She can tell people what to do and I would sit on a chair right by her door watching her take phone calls, answering questions and directing people in the office. She would let me pretend like I was her assistant and help her take notes, organize, shred papers, and do all the things in the office. I never thought of her as a working mother, I just thought of her as my mother.

I remember growing up and feeling like that's what I wanted to strive for in life.

I don't remember if this feeling was encouraged by my family or was internally motivated. Not only did I want to be like all the images of motherhood I had seen in society, but I felt I *should* be like them one day. So excited to be a mother. That there was nothing else more important for women other than being a mother and loving every minute of it. There was nothing in the media growing up about successful female leaders driving their way past social norms, having successful careers with no kids or both a successful career and kids. I knew my mom did it so why couldn't I?

I also had really good role models growing up who raised kids. I was so very fortunate enough to be a part of their journey in raising their kids. When my niece was born my mom and brother had her every weekend and I saw them take care of her. I saw what it took to get up at all hours of the night, change diapers, feed, dress, and love them to death. At this point I was only eight years old, and I felt so much love and appreciation for taking care of another human. My brother later had two more kids when I was a little bit older, and I was able to see him and his wife raise two adorable baby boys who are now in middle school and high school. I am currently around the age my brother and sister-in-law were when they had their babies which is so weird to think about.

I was also a babysitter for two different families through high school and college where I was able to see a strong role model for not only raising kids but also when taking a break and doing something for yourself was a priority. One was a fitness competitor and one opened her own business and franchised two companies! One of them used to call me the "baby whisperer" because I was able to get the babies to calm down and rest almost all the time. I loved those babies like they were my own and cannot believe one of them is now in high school! I was able to see how they were juggling motherhood and it seemed so easy. They seemed to have had it all.

Well, of course it seemed easy because I would come for a few hours, take care of the babies, love on them, and give them right back! I didn't see all the lonely or tiring nights where they were going through the trenches of motherhood. This was my first insight into seeing how mothers were taking care of themselves. Sometimes I would go over so that they could go to lunch and a movie with a friend. Sometimes it would be so they could volunteer. Sometimes it would be so that they could go to dinner with their husbands. Being there and seeing that they were taking time for themselves unapologetically so that they could be the best mothers, was such a blessing for me. It opened my eyes to the possibility of being your true self while being a mother, rather than just being a mother.

Even with so many amazing role models, I felt as though I needed to follow a "path" that had already been created for me. I didn't want to let my family down by doing what I really wanted to do or creating my own path. Having kids literally changed the course of my life and I'm not sure where I'd be if I didn't have them. But after going through this journey, I believe that becoming who you want to be is far more important than letting your family down.

Another extrinsic motivator in how my thought process developed with wanting kids, was growing up Catholic. I was exposed to a representation of purity where, being close to God, also meant being terrified God would shun you for doing anything sexual, let alone sex (especially sex outside of marriage). I remember being terrified to tell my family that I was moving out to live with my boyfriend at the time (now my husband) before we were married, because of the judgment I thought I would face.

But the second I did get married, there was so much pressure to hurry up and have kids. When we did get pregnant there was so much celebration around having a new baby.

And yet, in the early years, I was conflicted. Suddenly, I was no longer supposed to be fearful of losing God's love for having sex. It was as though that one piece of paper my husband and I had both signed, was supposed to flip a switch on my internal psyche. We were now one with God, and sex in marriage was celebrated! But this paradigm shift took me years to sort through with my husband and it was hard to free myself from all the guilt that came with sex, let alone having kids.

I am a Type A personality to the core.

I am very impatient. I will move to a shorter line in the grocery store if one is taking too long. I will honk at you if you are not going at a green light.

I am a high achiever. I graduated high school in the top fifteen students. I graduated with both my bachelors and master's within five years. I've always held a job. Always wanted the next best thing for myself. I am extremely competitive. If I lose in a card game, I will throw all the cards in the air. I will challenge anyone to a soccer match.

And because of it all, I am also extremely stressed.

My parents had high standards for me to the point where my mom made sure I got straight A's. My dad would rip my homework if it wasn't perfect and make me redo it. If I was a minute past curfew or on the phone too late, that was it. My life was over. On top of that, I have set very high standards for myself that are impossible to achieve. Never-the-less, up until this point, I had checked off all but one thing on my perfect little to-do-list of life.

Having kids.

As I waited for that pregnancy test to show the results, I could never have imagined what life-changing experiences would come next. As you could see in the photo at the beginning of this chapter, we took a picture the moment we found out we were pregnant. We look so ecstatic and happy, but looking back at the picture now it makes me want to cry. We had *no* idea what we were getting into, and nobody prepared us, even though we were married, homeowners, and loved each other. By society's standards we were prepared.

When we found out I was pregnant, our first thought was, now what? Should we feel different? Should we tell people? Do we call the doctor? Do we take five more at-home pregnancy tests to be sure? Do we start buying baby stuff? How early do I tell my boss? When did I last have a drink? I wonder how far along I am. I wonder if my dad is going to kill me because now, he knows I've had sex!

Even though my husband was with me when we saw the results, I instantly felt so alone. I felt like nobody understood what I was going through.

I was terrified that I wouldn't be able to spend quality time with my husband anymore, that my friends would all leave me, and my coworkers would think I was just a "mom." I was sad I wouldn't be able to travel as much anymore. I felt like I wasn't ready, even though we prepared for this. I felt like we should've waited longer. Even though I had taken all the steps society thought I needed—twenty-five years old, married, with a house and a job—I felt like my life was over and I couldn't tell anyone. I was happy but at the same time, I had all these negative feelings around being pregnant. Through my journey you will see that this is probably where my pre-partum began. In working a lot through therapy, I promise there is a light at the end of this tunnel.

Over time, it kind of felt like, when there is a small water leak at your house, and you don't notice it at first. The water begins seeping slowly away from the source to the rest of the house, until it erodes and causes greater damage. I was slowly slipping away, and being pushed farther and farther away from who I was.

We learned the first thing to do when you find out you're pregnant.

Call the doctor.

I called the doctor the next day and let them know that I needed to come in because I was pregnant.

Instantaneously the nurse said, "Congratulations!"

I immediately thought, *Wow, that was weird, what if I didn't want the baby? What if I had been raped? What if I didn't want to be "congratulated" for this weird thing growing inside of me?* But politely I said, "Thank you!" and went along with scheduling our first visit. I think medical professionals need to be a little more aware of what they say and how they say it. Such a small sentence can mean a lot of different things to different people.

Looking back, I'm not sure what instinct it was that made me call the doctor, because nobody tells you that you should call and make sure everything is okay. Maybe I learned it from shows or movies.

Sitting in the office for my initial appointment after finding out we were pregnant, waiting to be called in to the OBGYN (Obstetrician-Gynecologists who are the doctors that take care of your female parts) seemed like it would last forever. But the rest of the time was sort of a blur. They collected my urine in a small little cup. I was weighed and they told me everything looked fine. They had another doctor come in and talk about nutrition, exercise, what to eat and what not to eat but at a very high level. The doctor said, see you in four weeks and "bueno, bye!" I felt relief and excitement, fear, nerves, and also like the whole thing didn't seem real to me. There was no guide on what to do next.

Nobody told me that it is normal to wait to tell people you are pregnant because of the possibility of having a miscarriage. Twelve weeks is when they say you're in the "clear" to tell people, but there is always a possibility of it happening later in the pregnancy.

We didn't know this and told our family right away with all our pregnancies. With our first child, this was fine. But that wasn't the case with our second. For our second child, we bought little lottery cards that our family could scratch off and underneath it said we were pregnant. We were so excited, but little did we know, a few weeks later we would have a miscarriage.

I don't think it's necessarily a bad thing to tell people you are pregnant early on, but it's important to realize that if something happens, the phone calls and explanations you have to make after the fact will be burned in your memory forever.

Thank goodness my husband and I had faith that God knew what He was doing and why, even if we didn't. It was happening for a reason, and we just needed to trust in Him to make it through.

Back to the first pregnancy. My type-A personality immediately took over creating a checklist in my head.

We need to tell our parents.

We need to tell my boss.

We need to start getting the baby-room ready, planning the shower, and *all the things.*

In society, we have wedding planners, home organizers, travel agencies, but no help walking through pregnancy and giving birth. After doing a little research, I found there are a few companies out there who are trying to tackle this, but it's mostly for postpartum.

Why don't we have someone to hold our hand and walk us through the entire pregnancy and after giving birth, what to expect, things to think about, or even just FAQs. We have books but those are more like textbooks and who wants to read a textbook on what to expect. It's too daunting.

We have the option of having a doula or a midwife. A doula is someone who provides emotional, physical, and educational support for both parents to help them feel empowered to make informed decisions. A midwife is a medical professional trained to care for you during pregnancy, giving birth, and postpartum; they're available for exams and testing and support to deliver the baby during active labor. No one told me there were home visitors that do this. This is the time where you need to speak up and ask questions. Ask the doctor if there is someone you can talk more to about pregnancy, what to expect, any of your questions.

There is also the option to have a home visitor come to your home weekly and check up on you. In New Mexico, there are many options of having home visiting through hospitals, the county, nonprofit groups, and other organizations. It's important to know these options exist and to ask for them if you are interested. Home visitors are there to offer support and answer any questions you may have on things like prenatal care, sleep, self-care, nutrition, growth and development, and breast-feeding. Ask during your doctor's visits. Check your local free resources and see if it is available and free!

Nobody really offers them to you—you have to find them on your own or ask the doctor for a referral. But it is important to know they exist because your best advocate is you. Someone should make baby planning a thing and call it "**Mom**ents That Matter, Baby Planners." There's a huge gap in this industry that I think could be of great benefit!

"Pregnancy is really hard. After all you're trying to grow a whole other person inside of you which isn't easy. Yet, one of the hardest parts is actually realizing your life is about to change in a huge way but not knowing exactly how.
~Unknown"

CHAPTER 2

The Pregnancy Glow

I've heard a lot of people absolutely love being pregnant. The "pregnancy glow" they get, the long full hair, the magical feeling of growing another human inside you. The feeling inside that you are now becoming your "most full self" and fulfilling everyone's expectation of being a mother.

I was not one of those people.

Of course, that is not to say that some people don't have more traumatic or worse pregnancies either. I was sort of in the middle, caught in a purgatory between heaven and hell. However, before I go into the laundry list of things that sucked for me about being pregnant, I want to acknowledge those angel mama's who love being pregnant, thrive off it, and glow because of it. You women are so special, and I commend you for what you do and how you feel. Everyone is different and you never know how it's going to be until it happens. Although my pregnancies sucked in my eyes, let's dive right into the few little silver linings I found while being pregnant.

I saw something once that said we get maybe twelve times to play Santa, twelve spring breaks, thirteen first days of school, twelve easter baskets, twenty tooth fairy visits, one first date, two proms, one graduation, one chance to teach them to be good humans.

The days are really long but the years are short.

Did you know you don't usually get your period while pregnant? No pads, no tampons, no blood. Nada. It is so nice not having to worry about always having one on hand "just in case." On the other hand, some can have a period for nine months as well. There's also this thing called Premenstrual dysphoric disorder (PMDD) which is a severe form of PMS that can get worse after you have your baby each month you have your cycle.

Did you know some companies and stores have specific parking spots for pregnant women? It might not seem like a big win, but this is huge (pun intended) when you are nine months pregnant trying to shop for the baby and it's important to be close to a bathroom at ALL times.

Did you know your breasts can grow bigger when you get pregnant? You get to buy a whole new wardrobe and upgrade your bra situation. Megan Thee Stallion was not kidding when she said, "Body crazy, curvy, wavy, big titties, lil waist." I mean, for real. I've never looked so good in a shirt without a bra.

Did you know that you will be hungry all the time and literally can eat more than you ever have before. It's actually recommended that women eat an extra 300 calories per day when you are in the second and third trimesters!

Did you know your hair and nails grow super full and long when you are pregnant?

Did you know sex is so much better when you are pregnant. All the different positions you try because of your big belly being in the way, let's just say I was not complaining about this benefit..

All the eating you can do for "two" and not apologize. Yes!

Not to mention, it's just a miracle how the sperm meets the egg at just the right moment during your ovulation fertility window. For every little thing to fall into place, at just the right time, is amazing to think about.

It's even more amazing to think about your body being a vessel through which God sends a child to earth. A vessel that's able to give you all the things you need to keep that baby alive for the full nine months.

Not knowing anything about that baby, how it will look, what their personality will be like, how they will interact with you, what they will believe, how they will think, what their life will be like, is overwhelming to say the least. But know that you are in good hands. God chose you specifically to be this baby's parent, and to provide and support them through life is a feeling of joy that is unexplainable.

You can't truly understand the full extent of this until after the baby is here and your whole life has changed.

"Growing a baby makes me feel like a

A really tired, weak superhero who wants to eat all the time and is not allowed to lift heavy objects."
~Unknown

CHAPTER 3

Here we Grow

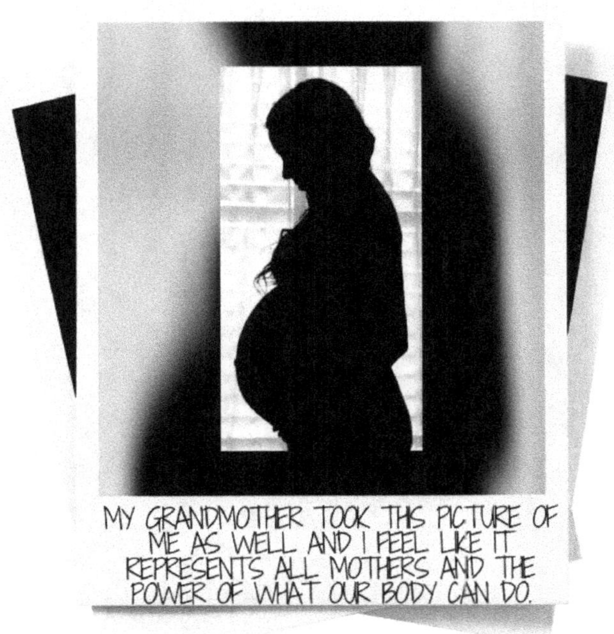

All those benefits aside, let me be clear I did not like being pregnant. There were so many side-effects I wasn't expecting, not to mention all the things I couldn't do. It was a major pain (pun intended).

Of course, every person is different and there are some who may have had none or possibly more than these symptoms, so this is just my experience. But I'm hoping to help anyone out there, who is even curious about pregnancy.

23

Mom

[ˈmʌðə] noun

One who sacrifices her sleep, body, sanity, social life, drinking hot coffee and peeing alone.

See also: "superwoman"

First Trimester

I DOCUMENTED EACH WEEK OF PREGNANCY SO I COULD LOOK BACK AND SEE THE GROWTH OF THE BABY. IT STILL DIDN'T FEEL REAL TO ME AT THIS POINT IN TIME.

I once heard that being pregnant was like running a marathon. Researchers studying the limits of human endurance have determined that the physical intensity of pregnancy is basically like running a 40-week marathon.

And it's true. You are tired all the freaking time. If you used to go to bed at 10:00PM, you are now done with the day around 8:00PM. And that's with naps in-between and dozing off in the car, at work, in the bathroom, basically anywhere you become still. Not much you can do about this, except to plan for it. You have bloating, gas, insomnia, acne, bleeding gums, vision loss, and back aches. Some people are even the "luckiest" to have morning sickness. And despite the name, it's not always in the morning. It can be literally all day and in all three trimesters but it's most common in the first few months of pregnancy.

Again, there is not much you can do about it other than eating small meals, ginger ale, and crackers. It can get bad to where you begin losing weight and fluids, so you have to go to the hospital to get checked out.

For my symptoms, my boobs started producing colostrum before I even had the baby, which is the first milk your breasts make in preparation for feeding your baby. Um…I was not prepared for this and literally had to wear pads in my bras so that I didn't leak all over. Thank goodness for my sister-in-law who gave me some hand me down pads because I had no idea that was even possible or that they even had pads specifically for this! If I had something pressed up against them like a tight shirt or sports bra, I would have been good for the entire day but the second I took it off, hello slow, drippy Niagara Falls.

It is also normal to gain weight during pregnancy, but the amount I gained was shocking to me. Depending on your body mass index, you could gain from 11 to 40 pounds! For context, a normal baby weight is between 5 and 13 pounds, so that's a lot of weight in your body not directly coming from the baby.

Some of the stranger symptoms I had were, gagging every time I brushed my teeth or put in my teeth night guard. Getting hot flashes at the most inopportune times. I also had weird pains every time I'd sit up quickly or get out of bed, or just turn sideways sometimes. It felt shooting pain, like I was being electrocuted in one little spot. Apparently, that's normal and called *Round Ligament Pain*. There are thick ligaments surrounding and supporting your uterus, and as the baby grows, that ligament stretches and separates. The doctor did end up telling me my pain was from this and there was not much you can do other than not making any sudden movements (which can be impossible with more than one child). Sudden moments can cause the ligaments to feel like God is thrusting his lightning bolt right into your side. In this case, lightning can strike twice.

Related to your vaginal area, the pressure of having a baby inside pushing your intestines around will make you pee all the time, even if I just took a sip of water. To make matters worse, your doctor tells you to drink 64 to 96 ounces of water a day. On the bright side, this helps you prepare for a baby since it makes you wake up every couple of hours at night to pee since you will be waking up every 2 hours to feed the baby once it's here. Along with peeing all the time, as you move into the next trimester, your lovely friend "pelvic pain" begins.

I only had pelvic pain during my first pregnancy, but it was bad. My doctor said it was probably because my uterus was growing faster than my body could handle, so every time I'd take a step, it would hurt. Now, you can purchase, which I did, a belly band to try to help take the weight off my pelvic bone, but it only helped while I had it on. It got so bad that I had to go to physical therapy to try to get help. Belly bands are a piece of fabric with Velcro that wrap around your waist and is adjustable to help lift the weight off your pelvis.

I don't remember what exercises they had me do, because I honestly blocked that whole thing out, but I do remember that it hurt, and I couldn't wait to get that baby out!

My second pregnancy I had what's called "lightning crotch." It's a sharp or shooting pain in your vagina or pelvis. Some people describe the pain as feeling like an electrical bolt or zap from the inside, which is where the condition gets its name.

Another thing that shocked me, was having to eliminate certain foods while pregnant because of potential bacteria: soft cheese, undercooked meat, fresh juice, sushi, raw cookie dough, homemade Caesar dressing, fresh pre-stuffed poultry, fish with mercury, meat spreads, unwashed fruits/veggies, raw sprouts, smoked seafood raw shell fish, basically anything raw, unpasteurized milk, not too much caffeine, alcohol of course, and the one that killed me the most, deli meats. However, did you know that some cheese and milk should have it on the label whether it's pasteurized in the U.S. or not and if it is pasteurized you are safe to eat it. I followed these rules in both my pregnancies because I was so worried about something happening to my babies. At this point is when my anxiety got a little worse.

You know the expression, "You always want what you can't have?" Well, I've never craved a fresh sandwich so bad in my life until I couldn't have deli meat. In fact, for my first post-labor meal, my dad brought me a Subway sandwich, and I scarfed that thing down so fast. It was almost the best meal of my life.

But getting used to all this also prepares you for all the things you have to worry about eating/drinking specific foods when you are breast-feeding as well. While nursing, you should watch your caffeine, limit fish high in mercury, herbal supplements, and highly processed food so it doesn't affect the baby. Caffeine can specifically keep the baby up just like it keeps you up! You should also avoid alcohol, of course, because it does transfer through the breastmilk. On multiple occasions I'd have a drink and then "pump and dump" as they call it. This is where you pump out the milk you produce for twenty-four hours until the alcohol has subsided in your body. Then you're safe to feed your baby again.

There are certain ultrasounds that happen during the 1st trimester and the first one is to determine your due date. I was so skeptical at first when they put us in a dark room, told me to pull up my shirt, pull down my pants and the doctor put slime all over me, then rubbed a very cold little instrument over my belly. But hearing the heartbeat for the first time was indescribable knowing that at that moment there is another life growing inside of you. When they gave me the due date I thought, how in the world do they know when I'm due based on the measurements of a tiny little pea on the screen? How do they know it's a baby and not my ovary? Do they know what they are doing?

Turns out yes, my baby was born one day from the original due date. The doctors do know what they're doing!

> I am not Buddha. Rubbing my pregnant belly will not bring you good luck, prosperity, or wealth.
> ~Unknown~

Second Trimester

WE WENT ON VACATION TO NEW YORK AS
OUR LAST HURRAH WE WERE ABLE TO
ANNOUNCE BEING PREGNANT ON GOOD
MORNING AMERICA WITH GINGER ZEE!

Now, it starts to feel a little more real. You have something growing inside of you. I've heard a lot of people say that having a baby is a miracle and it's so beautiful. Which don't get me wrong, I agree with. But personally, I just felt more like an alien was growing inside me and was trying its best to get out. This was a hard stigma to get over in society. I could tell everyone judged me when I was honest in answering their question of how excited or happy, I was. I think this also is where my anxiety got a little worse when I felt like I wasn't living up to everyone's "standards." I now know to screw the standards. Set your own and follow your "knowing."

And this is when the smack-in-the-face came for me, where I truly became aware of how this was going to affect me. It was like a sniper in the night, sneaking up on me quietly; you don't realize he's there until, boom! Your body starts changing and rearranging completely.

You begin to show stretch marks, no matter how many times you rub oil, cream, lotion, or magic potions. It gets a little harder to work out; where you may have been running the 1st trimester, you begin to take long walks instead. Your hip bones start spreading, and pants don't fit you right and you get bulges in places you never thought you could, so you either live in sweatpants and leggings or you have to use a hair tie around your button on your jeans to make them fit around your waist.

And then there's the kicking in your stomach from the baby. At first it felt like I was having hiccups in my stomach, but by 2nd trimester time, the hiccups turned into full-blown punching. It felt like my baby was doing a star-jump in my stomach and was trying to get out way too early. I remember having a conversation with a coworker in my cubicle, and she could literally see the baby tossing and turning in my stomach.

It was so uncomfortable I would push the baby as far down as I could. But both my kids were so stubborn they'd kick me back so hard it would hurt and tickle at the same time. Once again, people say it's such a miracle, and feeling the baby move is a joy, but I did not like it one bit.

Then there's something called diastasis recti where your ab muscles separate from pregnancy and if not treated can make your stomach stick out for years.

Yes—I said years.

Making sure you do the right exercises after pregnancy is so important to assist in the healing process, especially if you have a c-section. Laying on your back and doing toe taps on the ground will help. Why a new mother doesn't get to go to physical therapy after labor is beyond me. We suggest this for major surgeries, but not for after giving birth.

During pregnancy you're not allowed to lay on your stomach for obvious reasons of not hurting the baby. You're also not supposed to lay on your back. You are, however, able to work out with the same intensity you were working out when you got pregnant. This is great except that for my first child, when I got pregnant, I had just gotten over a broken ankle and wasn't able to exercise because of that. So, during my entire pregnancy I wasn't able to work out like I was used to, and I think that really did a number on my mental health. Especially when I was used to using exercise as an outlet to release my anxiety.

In between all the preparing, the best piece of advice I could give is:

Get a massage.

Get a massage, early and often. Find a place that has a special pregnancy massage table where you can lay on your stomach on the table with a hole in it for your belly! Make someone give you a massage. It was amazing and I've never felt more relaxed. This can also help with hip and back aches due to pregnancy. This is something you take for granted being pregnant. Laying on your stomach!

A test that the doctors complete in the 2nd trimester is a glucose test. It's usually conducted between 24 and 28 weeks of pregnancy. Abnormal glucose levels may indicate gestational diabetes. So, the doctors have you drink a super sweet solution, and have you give blood where they monitor those glucose levels. I've heard drinking this not so tasty solution is hard for people (especially if you have morning sickness), but if you chug it like you're at the club, no problems!

It's interesting to talk through the different types of tests because throughout the pregnancy, as your baby grows you will have numerous ultrasounds. There are some that measure for any abnormalities or defects with the baby, to diagnose an unusual pregnancy or miscarriage, and also to examine the pelvic anatomy. Each one caused me to have a little more anxiety each time we went because it's hard to know what to expect. All you can do is pray that the baby is happy and healthy.

Having a support system during this time was pivotal for me. Having my husband tell me that everything will be fine no matter what, made all the difference.

But whether you have all the support in the world or no support at all, you can still have something called perinatal mood and anxiety disorders. I honestly didn't even know this was a thing until my youngest was three years old. These anxiety disorders include perinatal obsessive-compulsive disorder (OCD), perinatal panic disorder, and perinatal psychosis. Some risk factors for these disorders are familial history of depression, anxiety, or mood disorders, fertility treatments, multiple births, lack of sleep and having baby in the neo-intensive care unit.

A lot of people have heard of postpartum depression but perinatal disorders are a whole new ball game. These can happen while you are pregnant not just after you have the baby. Most of the time you don't realize what it is until it gets so bad, you're not sure what to do. This could look like constant worry, feeling like something bad is going to happen, racing thoughts, appetite and sleep disturbances, inability to sit still, and physical symptoms like nausea, dizziness, and hot flashes.

It's important for all of us to recognize the signs and get help when it's needed.

You can ask your provider for a referral to someone.

You can contact the National Suicide and Crisis Lifeline for emergencies by dialing 988 or 911.

You can contact the Postpartum Support International Help line at 800-944-4773.

You can contact the National Maternal Mental Health Hotline at 833-943-5746.

You can contact a home visitor program.

You can share your story.

Let's kick that door of stigma in and begin to help ourselves and others heal by not making this a taboo subject and speaking openly about it.

Let's save lives one share at a time!

You are not alone out there!

There are a lot of resources that can help, and they may look different for everyone. It could be attending a support group, getting medication, therapy, community support, Facebook groups, mom apps, and literally a little sleep. Whatever it may be, please don't be afraid to ask for help and trust your intuition that something is wrong.

And it doesn't have to be that something is always wrong for you to receive support. If you are a type A personality like me and think you should or can do everything once you have the baby, I'm here to tell you it's impossible and you will drive yourself crazy trying to do it all.

In my circumstance, when I was in the middle of my emotions after having my baby, I was lucky enough to have my family come over and watch the baby while I was at work. When I would come home, the dishes would be done, the laundry would be folded, and the house would be clean.

And guess what, I did not like it one bit. How dare they try to help me! How dare they do things for me that I should be doing.

It was like a slap in the face at the time where I internalized it, and it made me feel like I wasn't capable or not meeting everyone's unrealistic expectations. I felt like they were telling me I wasn't being good enough. I wish someone would've sat down and talked to me about this whether it be my doctor, family, or friends. I wanted—no I needed—someone to tell me please accept the help. Any and all help. And it doesn't mean you are not enough, or a capable mother, or lazy. It just means that it's going to be hard. Letting others help you, will make a huge difference and your mental health is more important than folded laundry or a clean kitchen sink. I promise. I saw something once that said post-partum is like taking your final exam on the first day of class, and you don't even know what class you are in, and the exam is in another language, and everyone is crying! Just like when the baby is crying and gets heavy, you set them down. When society's expectations get heavy, I'm here to tell you it's okay to put them all down and focus on the present.

So again, if someone offers to help, let them help so you can pass the exam!

To those that may not be a parent but are part of a support system whether that be through an organization, a church, friends, or family…

SHOW UP.

Let me say that again for the people and families that are in the parent's life.

SHOW UP!

Send the parents flowers.

Better yet, set up meal trains online and/or send or take food to the family after the baby's born for the first few weeks.

Give the parents a gift for the baby's first birthday rather than getting a baby a toy they'll never play with.

Visit, do their dishes, laundry, floors, heck even let the parent take a shower or a nap.

Text them to let them know you're thinking of them and that they are a great parent.

Provide them with an ear to just listen and not judge or give advice.

Send them resources if they might need it.

Ask them how their day was or if they want to hear about what's going on at work.

Show up and go on a walk with them.
Take their other child outside for a bit.

Whether you know it or not, showing up matters.
You never know when you might be saving a life.

There is a lot of people in your life that will want to be around you when times are good; when you go out to dinner, travel together, go to concerts together, go dancing together, but the ones who stay by your side when you are falling apart and have nothing to offer are the people who truly support and love you.

"Months have an average of **30** days except the 9th month of pregnancy which has about **1000** days."
~Unknown

Third Trimester

36 WEEKS PREGNANT WITH MY DAUGHTER. MY SON WAS SO EXCITED, ALMOST AS EXCITED AS I WAS NOT TO BE PREGNANT ANYMORE!

This is the time where I began "nesting."

I was getting anxious about the baby coming and I began to clean everything in sight. I folded the clothes and put them into drawers (adding a dryer sheet to keep them fresh), planned my baby shower, and started organizing everything. Nesting during pregnancy is an old wives' tale that once it begins, labor is about to come. It's basically an overwhelming desire to get your home ready for your new baby.

One thing people did warn me about was that I wouldn't have time to do anything when the baby came. But it was right around this time that I found myself with not a lot to do. So, I started researching everything. I had a whole Pinterest board of everything I needed to know and didn't want to forget. One of them was about what to pack in your "go bag" for the hospital. I think I was so nervous about having everything that I had it packed when I was seven months pregnant. Who knew you would have to pack like you're going on a trip for two, just to have your child at the hospital.

Thank God for these boards. I found so much helpful information. You may not need all of these things, but they are a good reminder for things you may forget. Some of the things that stand out to me that were super helpful were:

Snacks: Good for both mom and dad because you can never count when the hospital would bring you food or how long it would take. You will need this as you begin breast-feeding as well.

Chargers: Keep your phones charged up so you can let everyone know the baby has arrived and take pictures!

Baby car seat, clothes, and diaper bag: They won't let you leave without knowing you have a car seat ready, so I would suggest carrying it in with you when you first go to the hospital, so your significant other doesn't have to go running to the car before you leave. Make sure it's installed (before you go into labor) and that you know how to buckle and unbuckle it.

Baby clothes & Diapers: Now, you don't really need clothes for the baby since the hospital provides a little onesie, but if you want an outfit for pictures, go for it. I don't think you need a diaper bag either because the hospital gives you plenty of diapers/wipes/blankets for the baby, so there's not much you actually need in the diaper bag until you get home. I didn't know this and the first baby we took a fully stocked diaper bag. Turns out it was just another bag we had to carry since we didn't end up using anything from it.

Work paperwork for the Family and Medical Leave Act (FMLA): FMLA is a federal labor law that entitles eligible employees to take unpaid, protected leave for family and medical reasons while continuing group health insurance. Remember any forms you need the doctor to fill out for FMLA so they can fill it out right then and there. That way you don't have to worry about faxing/emailing requests or trying to get ahold of someone. This was super helpful.

It is a luxury for women to have an employer in the United States provide time off, let alone paid time off. America is one of only six countries in the world without paid leave and 1 in 4 mothers have had to return to work within two weeks of giving birth. And leading the way is Bulgaria—offering 58 weeks of paid maternity leave. Globally, the average paid maternity leave is 29 weeks, and the average paid paternity leave is 16 weeks. Make sure you fully understand your employers' rules and policies around time off to ensure you are clear on paid or unpaid time off.

Advanced Healthcare Directive: An advance

healthcare directive also known as a living, will, is a legal document that specifies what actions should be taken for your health if you are no longer able to make decisions for yourself due to illness or incapacity. Hopefully, you will never need this, but there are so many different complications that can happen with labor that it's good to have it on hand after having that conversation with your spouse or your support.

Headphones/Music: This really helped me get through labor because there are so many beeping noises, nurses checking on you, the TV, your significant other and so many other things going on. I put on my headphones and tried to go to my happy place with the only song that ever calms me down, "Hallelujah" by Kate Voegele.

Clothes and underwear: I didn't realize until my second child that I could buy my own maternity hospital gown to wear after. This doesn't really matter, but it's more comfortable and stylish than the gross one they give you at the hospital. I wore the gross one until I had the baby, got cleaned up and then changed to the other. This was also super helpful with breast-feeding because it has little areas to open for feeding.

You'll also need a comfortable pair of clothes and undies to go home in. You'll want to be as comfortable as possible because you will be sore, tired, and possibly cold like I was when you have your baby in the winter. The hospital will give you this mesh underwear to wear with a pad so that it helps with the bleeding. Who knew that I would be coming home in a diaper as well as my baby.

You won't be in your normal clothes for a very long time after giving birth. You may feel like you want to throw out all your old clothes because they don't fit but don't throw out your maternity clothes! You'll still need your breast-feeding bras for years to come. I ended up keeping mine for a while because even though I wasn't breast-feeding, my ribs expanded, and I had to use bra extenders for my regular bras. Breast-feeding bras are just a little more comfortable. I actually ended up buying this brand called Ollie Gray bras because they were so comfy and good for exercising in.

Going back to the birth, I remember wondering if my water was going to break or not (for some women the doctors have to break it) and being so scared it would happen at work. In fact, I ended up wearing a pad that last week "just in case" so I wouldn't be embarrassed. Luckily, I went into labor at night and didn't have to worry about it.

My first baby was breech, meaning the baby's feet were positioned in a way to come out first. So, I had to bounce on a yoga ball and do yoga poses to flip the baby a week before labor. Thank goodness he ended up flipping in the right direction otherwise I most likely would've had to have a c-section. A c-section creates a whole new set of issues for mothers!

By this time in my pregnancy, I felt huge. Like, so huge that every step I took was painful on my pelvis. It felt like I was carrying fifty pounds on my stomach alone. My back hurt, my feet hurt, my stomach hurt and to top it all off, everywhere I turned people felt like they had the right to comment on my appearance.

"Oh wow, you must be close!"

"You don't look big at all."

"You look like you're going to bust!"

They also commented a lot on the gender of my child.

"Oh, you're carrying low, I bet you it's going to be a boy!"

They even commented on how I was still working.

"I can't believe you're still here!"

I know it was coming (mostly) from a loving place, but when did it become okay to comment on another person's appearance, just because they're pregnant? I don't go around commenting on everyone who has gained weight, or isn't wearing makeup that day, or that got a haircut that looks ridiculous.

Not one time in my life have I heard someone ask a male why they were at work because their wife just had a baby. It's not only celebrated, but expected, for males to be working through pregnancy and right after the birth of their baby. Why is it any different for a female who is carrying the baby, to not be at work? It's as though she has lost all her qualifications because she is pregnant.

If anything, she should be given more qualifications and be celebrated for continuing to work up to giving birth. Not only do you have to put up with everyone's drama at work—responsibilities, deadlines, meetings—but you also have to make sure you eat and drink enough, make sure you exercise, make sure you rest, all while growing a human being inside of you and sometimes not feeling so great.

This was also around the time where people thought it was okay to randomly touch my belly. Nothing prepared me for how a complete stranger thought it was okay to not only comment on my life but go in straight for the belly rub.

It was like an action movie where the scene was a slow motion shot of the stranger's hand moving toward my belly. The music begins to climax and then I swat their hand away and start telling them, "Who do you think you are, that you think you can just touch me whenever you feel like it!"

Of course, that was in my head and I mostly, politely told people not to touch me (and sometimes not so politely swat their hand away). A few times I'd say, "If you didn't put it there, you cannot touch it."

"EMOTIONALLY,
I AM DRAINED.
MENTALLY,
I AM WEAK.
SPIRITUALLY,
I AM DOUBTFUL.
PHYSICALLY,
I AM IN PAIN."
~UNKNOWN

CHAPTER 4

Nauseous, Exhausted, Overjoyed

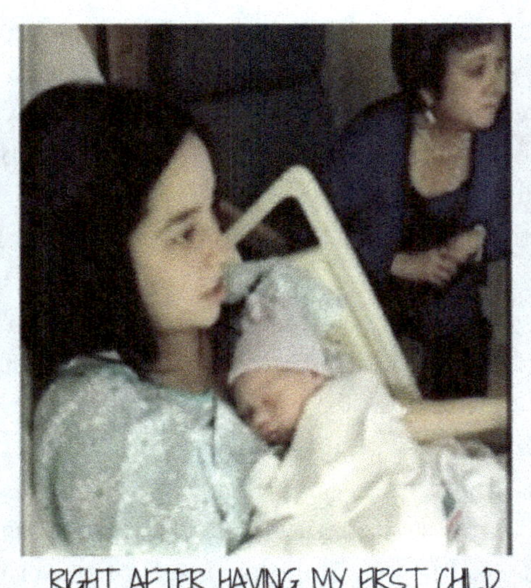

RIGHT AFTER HAVING MY FIRST CHILD.
GETTING BONDING TIME WITH MY PROUD
MOM IN THE BACKGROUND.
ALSO, ME TERRIFIED OF HAVING A KID.

Never in my mind would I have imagined that being pregnant would be such a torturous thing. It takes over your body, chews it up with all the crazy things that happen during, and spits it out in the aftermath of having the baby.

Case in point, I have always been athletic. I played soccer and basketball in school, have completed triathlons, run half marathons and a full marathon and yet, labor was the most painful thing I had ever been through.

A week before I went into labor, my mom tried to warn me. She was so worried about how painful it was going to be, and I sort of shrugged it off thinking, okay mom, we have very different pain tolerances and I'm younger and in better shape than you were when you were younger. Even after she told me I didn't understand, I told her not to worry, I would be okay, and that was that.

Everyone had questions about my birth plan, whether I was going to get an epidural, where I was going to give birth, the due date, on and on and on. Building a birth plan, luckily, was easy for my husband and me. We wanted to give birth in a hospital in case anything went wrong and because I knew I wanted—wait, scratch that— needed an epidural. Why go through all that pain if you don't have to? Between 60-70% of pregnant people get epidurals for pain management but success rates vary on if they even work. It depends on different things like the anatomy of the mother, the placement of the epidural, and the position of the baby. Experts say that it's a good idea to get to know other pain management techniques just in case the epidural doesn't work.

There are so many different ways you can choose to set up a birth plan. There is the location and type of birth you will have. For example, there is a vaginal birth with an epidural, there is a natural vaginal birth without any medication either at the hospital or in your own home, there is a water birth where you have the baby in water, there is a scheduled induction and c-section if your doctor orders those.

I don't want to go without saying that there are ways to set up a birth plan if you are planning to have a baby yourself but there can also be many different ways to have a baby as well. There is in vitro fertilization commonly known as IVF. This is a technique that helps people with fertility problems have a baby. They remove an egg from the woman's ovaries and fertilize it in a lab to make an embryo and then return it to the womb to grow and develop. The percentage of live births from IVF is 55.6%.

There is also adoption where you adopt a baby that someone else has already been born. There is lots of information on this for the process as it's different in each state. You can have a closed adoption, which means there is no contact between the birthparents and the adoptive parents of the child. You can also have an open adoption where all parties remain in each other's lives after the adoption as well. The average cost of adoption is between $30,000 and $60,000.

Another way to have a baby is via surrogacy. This is where you plan a pregnancy via medical procedure like IVF but in this case the doctor places the embryo from the intended mother and father into another person to grow. The intent of surrogacy is if a woman is unable to become pregnant for many different reasons. The average cost of surrogacy is around $100,000. Each is different and unique in their own ways. It's amazing to think of how far science has come to be able to give someone something that they might not be able to have naturally.

Back to those who are giving birth themselves. There are so many different things to think about when giving birth, who is going to be in the room with you, what music will you want to listen to, do you want photos or video, do you want to try different positions, do you want dim lighting, do you want a massage, reflexology, essential oils, etc. It's basically a plan of how you think your childbirth should go and any special decisions or circumstances you want to share with your doctor. It's important to note that there are many different birthing plans you can choose from, and which ones are right one for you. Mine didn't go 100% as planned but the only plan is the baby's plan.

Nobody else, other than my mother, mentioned the sweet-baby-Jesus-pain I would go through to push that baby out. I did hear a few times that "Oh you know, any pain you might feel disappears the moment you meet the baby."

Um, no.

The pain doesn't go away, and it might even get worse after the baby is out. It's good to point out at this time how powerful and amazing women are. In the case that you do have to give birth naturally it's good to know that the human body can endure 45 units of pain but during childbirth a woman endures up to 57 units of pain equivalent to twenty fractures simultaneously!

We are definitely rockstars!

Did you know while breast-feeding, your uterus contracts after the baby is born! I sure didn't, but we'll get into that a little bit later. After you have the baby, it hurts to sit down, it hurts to breathe, it hurts to hold the baby, everything hurts. Yes, having the baby is a miracle and some may forget the pain, but I did not. The pain hit me like a full force semi-truck slamming into me without time to push any brakes.

I recently lost my grandmother, and although she was my last living grandparent, I never felt so undeniably heartbroken. Maybe it was because I wasn't very old when my other grandparents passed away and didn't really have a chance to comprehend what was happening, as I do now. She was the one person I could talk to about anything or anyone and she would never hold any judgment. I always told her my secrets—and anything I told her—was safe with her. She was *my* "person," the one I could call any time of day (literally 5:00AM to 10:00PM). She would answer, be awake, and be so grateful and happy to hear my voice.

I never took her for granted, and as she began to age, and I had my two kids, I tried my hardest to visit and talk to her as much as I could. We would watch shows like Dancing with the Stars and The Bachelor and then call each other after to gossip about what we thought about the eliminations, or who we wanted to win, or even who she thought was the cutest! Drinking our tea, we woke up at the crack of dawn to watch Meghan and Harry get married at Windsor Castle.

So, you can imagine, when I got the call one morning that she was on the way to the hospital, I was hopeful it was just a small medical incident, and I could talk to her soon.

Little did I know I was going to have to go through one of the most painful couple of months in my life while also navigating the subject of death with my kids.

My heart felt like an elephant was sitting on it, and I was on the verge of a panic attack every day. I couldn't breathe. Any little thing that related to her, any thought I had about her, set me off. But I felt like I had to leave the room and get all my tears out, so I didn't freak out my kids.

My head hurt, my body hurt, I really didn't want to get out of bed or go to work.

Death has always been such a frustrating thing for me, not understanding how someone could be here one second, and not the next. I believe in God, and I know he has a plan I don't know about, and I have faith that she is in heaven with my other grandparents, but it still doesn't make it any easier. I would, and still have, very vivid dreams about her comforting me and the kids telling us she's okay and it's okay, everything will be fine and that she's with my grandpa "the love of her life" as she would say in my dream.

You might think this is beautiful and I'm lucky to have such vivid dreams of her but when you wake up after a dream like this and it takes you a second to realize it was just a dream, it makes you feel like you lost her all over again. All the pain I thought had passed, comes rushing back and I lose it in a pile of my tears until I can catch my breath, or my husband wakes me up.

I hadn't lost anyone close to me in a very long time, and I had no idea how to navigate this now having my kids. I knew that I needed to stay present in everything I was doing to try to remind myself I cannot control the past or the future.

We received great advice:

"Just tell them the truth. She had something happen in her brain to make her stop breathing and now is in heaven."

So, my husband and I sat down our oldest in our bed and told him just that. I was trying my hardest not to cry and keep it together, but I told him the facts, told him "Mommy is very sad and might be crying, but to know that grandma is in a better place and loved him very much." I wasn't sure how he was going to react because he is a very sensitive four-year-old. He just looked at us and said, "Okay mom, she's in heaven with Jesus so it's okay."

That melted my heart and reminded me to think like a child and have child faith in God.

He also had very vivid dreams about her and told me he held her hand while he was having nap time at school. I guess he gets that from me, and of course sometimes he sees something that reminds him of her and gets really sad and starts crying that he "wants grandma." I just held him until he stopped and let him know I miss her too but she's always with us in one way or another and loves us so much.

It's a never-ending battle as I'm sure anyone who has lost someone knows, but over time it does get better and having faith that I will one day see her again soothes my soul like nothing else could.

I know you might be asking what this story has to do with giving birth. I wasn't really prepared to write about this story, but I think that feeling when you lose someone you love—that heart-aching, panicky, can't breathe, and can't go on any longer, kind of pain—is very similar in my mind to how labor feels.

But instead of being the emotional loss of a loved one, it's much more physical. I have tried to think about so many different analogies to explain it, but the one thing I think comes close is to think about it like having a blood pressure cuff around your entire mid-section (boobs to pelvic bone) and that cuff is the strongest cuff you've ever felt. And not only does that cuff squeeze you, but it also has electric nodes attached to it, the ones that you use to stimulate your muscles. There goes the blood pressure cuff, God presses the go button, and you can't breathe for the minute that it's squeezing, and then it releases, and you feel like, "Okay, maybe I can get through this, this isn't that bad."

Just as you catch your breath from the contraction, God says, just kidding, I'm not done yet and BOOM, they just keep on coming harder and stronger. I know, right about now you may want to shut the book, throw up your hands, and say, "Forget it. I'm not having kids. I can't imagine myself going through all of this!"

But it's important to remember, each story is different, and each labor is different. I hope that you continue and have faith in yourself, that you can do it!

You were literally made to do it!

In the end you may not forget all the pains once the little bundle of joy enters the world, but it is worth it. The joy and happiness you will feel when you are able to say they are mine and I am theirs. They are loaned to you from God. When you get the best hugs. When they say I love you mommy. And when you kiss them goodnight in hopes they will change the world one day.

It is all worth it.

"We have a secret in our culture, and it's not that birth is painful. It's that women are STRONG."

~Laura Stavoe Harm

CHAPTER 5

Someone new is Joining the Crew

I believe preparing for labor is just as important as being in labor.

Some people hire doulas or midwives to help with the labor. Some people get a chiropractic adjustment before the baby to ensure everything is in alignment to help with a smooth delivery. Some people get a Brazilian wax before so all the blood spewing out of you after the delivery doesn't make more of a mess with your hair in your vaginal area. Some people practice meditation or yoga to focus on breathing to help with breathing through labor. Some people take child-birthing classes to help prepare for labor, delivery, postpartum, and breast-feeding. Some people take a tour of the hospital to know where to go when you go into labor. Some people stock up on supplies and food like their doomsday prepping because they know they won't want to do anything after delivery. Some people set up the nursery, fold the baby clothes, build the crib, test out the rocking chair, and buy all the diapers. Some people have sex or eat pineapples to try to go into labor. Some people walk miles a day just to see if it will help speed up the labor. Some people eat dates and raspberry leaf tea, so they'll have a smoother labor (this actually softens your cervix and allows the birth to be a lot smoother and lessens the chance of your vagina tearing). Some people totally freak out with the unknown of all that encompasses being called "mommy."

And by some people, I mean me.

I am some people.

The first pregnancy I was so worried about knowing when to go to the hospital. I didn't want to have the baby naturally without an epidural, or at home, but I also didn't want to look like a fool if I went to the hospital and wasn't ready. So, my doctor told me at one of my last checkups about the 5-1-1 rule. If the contractions come every "5" minutes, lasting "1" minute each, for at least "1" hour, get to the hospital. Of course, if your water breaks, this is also a sign to get to the hospital immediately. Especially if it's been more than 24 hours since your water breaks and you are under 37 weeks pregnant. In most cases some doctors will want you to deliver within 48 hours of your water breaking, but that depends on a lot of things that you'll need to talk to your doctor about like, how far along you are and your medical history. When you are with your doctor, ask questions. Ask any questions you might have even if you think they are dumb because they are there to help you.

So, for my first pregnancy, when I started feeling contractions, I told my husband we needed to go to the hospital. He started driving to the hospital and I was pissed because he decided this was the day to go five miles an hour down the freeway (at least it sure felt that way). We get to the hospital, and I walk up to the check-in nurse and tell her I think I'm having contractions and she kind of laughs a little and says, "If you were having contractions, you would know." They checked me all out and turns out I was just having what's called Braxton Hicks!

Braxton Hicks are fun little false-labor pains. They don't usually appear until the latter part of your pregnancy and they're just your body's way of preparing for labor. These pains are usually not as bad as normal labor pains, but it still feels like that blood-pressure cuff tightening and loosening. But they're not consistent and they usually do go away after drinking water and laying down. A couple of things that can make them worse are physical activity and dehydration. So, turns out one of my fears came true that I made a fool of myself by not knowing the difference. But I was okay and you are entitled to 'not know'. The nurse was right though, you will for sure know when you are in labor.

For my second pregnancy, I started getting contractions in the early evening. I knew they were different because they were really painful, and I literally couldn't move when they started. I would have to focus on my breathing to get through it and they did, for sure, get worse and longer.

At one point, someone told me to eat a huge meal before I go to the hospital because once you get there and they start giving you medications, you aren't allowed to eat until after the birth. This was true, and I was starving the whole time with my first. So, with my second, I was going prepared.

I told my husband I wanted food from a popular Mexican restaurant in our city, Garcia's. He looked at me like I was crazy because I was in labor! But I told him I just want one more dinner as a family, with that specific food, and I wanted it now. So, after we debated back and forth a few times whether it was worth it to go, we went.

The food was so, so, good and I remember having contractions in the middle of eating. The poor waiter taking our drink order looked at me and then at my husband like "You better get her out of here, she's going to pop" We barely made it through the dinner because my son, who was three at the time, ate the slowest he ever had. It was like he was savoring those pancakes because he knew this was the last meal of peace and quiet.

We finally got home, and I finally felt like I had the energy to give birth. Luckily, I had my aunt and uncle on call to come over and watch our first kid! They came within the hour, and we were off.

The contractions were so bad my husband had to drive me to the front of the hospital, and someone had to bring me a wheelchair as I waited for him to park the car and take me to the check-in station. It's good to ask someone when you get there where the labor and delivery floor is. Better yet, take a tour of the hospital before so you know exactly where to go. It felt like eternity waiting there in that wheelchair, but it was probably no more than a few minutes.

There were so many times through my pregnancy and labor that I kept telling myself, if all these women throughout the world can do it before me, I can do it too. That's probably the only thing that kept me going.

"You won't remember what someone **said,** you won't remember what someone **did,** but you will remember how someone **made you feel."**

-Maya Angelou

CHAPTER 6

Push it, Push it real good

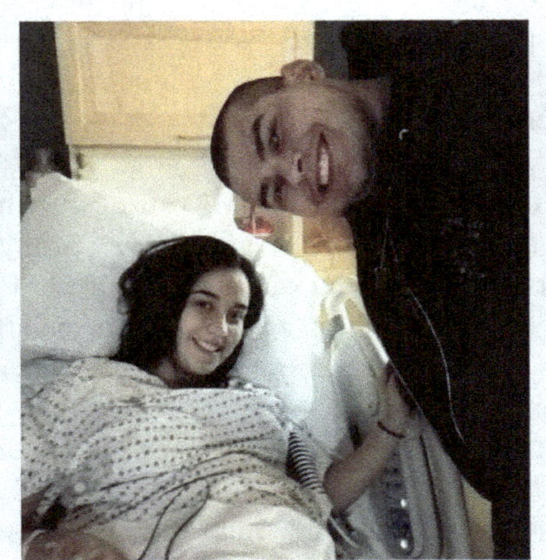

I'm going to tell you the story of my first delivery because my second one was pretty much a breeze and that's boring and uneventful (but also should give you hope)!

My first was a doozie, and although I didn't have any complications or a C-section like others may have, it was a horrible experience for me from birth to about one year after.

The check-in nurse took us to a private room and told me to change into the hospital gown after which he proceeded to check the degree of dilation of my cervix. This process has always been weird to me, even though I understand there probably isn't any other way to check. But it's basically having the nurse insert their fingers into your vagina to check to see if your cervix is opening. This becomes extremely awkward and uncomfortable when your husband is sitting next to you and get this, the nurse is a guy.

At the time, I didn't care because I was in so much pain, but thinking back after the birth, it was uncomfortable for me so I can't imagine how my husband felt. How do they not jump across the bed and strangle the dude? Luckily mine is in the medical field so he knew the guy just had to do his job.

Anyway, I think I was only 2 centimeters dilated, nothing crazy, but it hurt like hell, and they told me they couldn't give me an epidural until I was 4 centimeters. This is the time they may also give you fluids through an IV in your hand, wrist, or arm. This can also be really painful depending on the needle size, how small your veins are, and how experienced the nurse is. They put this little band around my stomach to monitor the baby's heartbeat and gave me some medicine to speed up the process. We hoped it would work otherwise I would've had to have a C-section. By this time, we had a bigger private room where we both set up camp. Don't ask me how we got there because I don't remember if they wheeled the bed, wheeled me in a wheelchair or if I was able to walk. All I remember is sitting there going through the pain and squeezing my husband's hand with every contraction that came. Having someone as support made a huge difference for me to know I was not alone.

The first nurse we had, Adriana, was so sweet and nice. I don't remember what she looked like, but I just felt a connection with her, and she made me feel at peace like everything was going to be ok. She talked me through everything that was supposed to happen, was happening, and had yet to happen.

I think back now, and she was for sure my guardian angel. She would sit there with me at almost every contraction and hold my hand, she'd tell me how well I was doing and reminded me to breathe. She'd go do her rounds and then come back to the room as soon as she could. Maybe it was because she was such a good nurse, but maybe it was because she could see the terror in my eyes of having my first child and not knowing what in the world I was doing.

I finally hit 4 centimeters and they asked if I wanted an epidural. Of course, I said yes; it was always in the birth plan to have one, because there was no reason for me to do it naturally. I have so much respect for those mama's who do it naturally and handle it like a boss but, I'll pass on that one. The anesthesiologist came in and gave me my first epidural, yes, I said first. I didn't know what to expect but the first thing they told me was my husband had to leave because it was technically a surgical procedure. Um, hello. Who knew that this was a medical procedure and that you couldn't have any support during this time.

Why didn't anybody warn me that my support person would have to leave for me to go through more pain? I'm not sure how long it took but that was my first glimpse of hope to have the pain literally go numb. They put you in this weird position on the side of the bed crouched over like the Hunchback of Notre Dame and tell you to breathe, regardless of if you're in the middle of a contraction or not. This, my friends, was not easy. It's hard enough to breathe through a contraction, yet alone crouch over like you don't have a huge belly. They get a super long needle—which I did not look at so that I didn't psych myself out—and then insert it into your spine. I waited, and waited, and waited until about ten minutes went by, and I asked the nurse, "Am I supposed to be feeling everything still?"

She looked at me like I was crazy and said, "You feel everything still?!"

I said, "Yes, everything, I don't feel any change."

She went to go get the anesthesiologist right away and they looked at the needle and said it probably wasn't in the right place and asked if I wanted another one.

I said, "YES!"

So, they proceeded to give me my second epidural, and yet again I say second because we are not quite done. This one felt a little different and I could feel half of my body go numb, a little bit of my feet, but I could still feel my entire stomach and every contraction.

At this point, I could tell the nurse was a little bit scared, but she tried to reassure me she would get someone in there again. I don't remember what time it was, but I do know that a shift change had happened for the anesthesiologist. It's possible I had gotten a new person in training, but there was no guarantee that the person taking over would know what they were doing.

By this time, I was 8 centimeters dilated, and they said if I wanted an epidural, I would need to do it quick. I said, "Well, they better freakin' hurry because this is the third one!" The nurse did everything she could to get them in as fast as possible and thank God for her.

I know I was so lucky to have her by my side, and I think she felt a connection as well because it was way past her shift change, and she chose to stay with me until I had the baby. This angel of a woman chose to stay with me…for hours after she could've gone home, stayed with someone she barely met, to ensure I was taken care of and to see the little baby she had been taking care of for me. God bless her.

Up until this point, I had occasionally watched Doctor Oz. on T.V. for some helpful information on how to stay healthy during pregnancy. Maybe having it on in the background while I'm cooking or reading. But watching his show while you're going through labor is probably not the best idea. I remember I had the T.V. on for background noise and distraction in the delivery room. I was so irritated with the Doc that I told my husband to turn it off because I was sick of hearing his voice. To this day, I cannot watch Dr. Oz without having P.T.S.D.

I don't know why, but I never got mad at my husband. I've heard there's a temptation to get mad at your support person for "doing this to you," but I never did. I truly felt like he was part of me and understood what I was going through, even though he wasn't physically going through it himself. There were some times he would look at me like I was a crazy person because my face would turn red, I'd stop breathing, and my legs would shake, but I knew he was on my side. I know that I was lucky to have support and realize not everyone might have this.

I could tell we were getting close to pushing because more people kept coming into the room and checking on us. I was super lucky enough to have my OBGYN on shift that night and she was able to deliver our baby. I never even thought that it was in question that your own doctor would not be the one delivering your baby, but apparently it happens. I'm not sure why it didn't snap, but I felt like, why would you go to the same doctor for nine months only to leave it up to chance on whether they were working the day you go into labor?

But luckily, she was there, and the team of nurses came in and prepared everything for delivery. They rolled out a cart, laid out their surgical instruments, put on their surgical gloves on, and told me it was time to push. I saw all the tools laid out on the table and the true crime junkie in me immediately thought "Oh no, this was a trick, they're going to cut me open and chop me up into tiny pieces and then I'll be dead."

By this time, I didn't feel the contractions anymore, thank the Lord, so it was easier to push when a contraction came. I also didn't realize that you end up pushing during the contraction instead of before or after. But it makes sense because the contraction is basically trying to squeeze the baby out and so you are trying to help your body by pushing during the contraction. This was tons of fun, not!

They made me take a deep breath and push for ten seconds. I mean what's ten seconds, right? Wrong, it felt like a whole minute each time. For my delivery, I was lucky to only be pushing for about forty minutes. But it went by so fast it felt like five minutes. I pushed and pushed until my little heart felt like it would explode and then they told me I wasn't breathing enough so they had to put an oxygen mask on me to ensure the baby was getting enough oxygen.

Also, side note, did you know that it's normal to poop while in labor? Who knew? But it is a real-life thing. It didn't happen to me, but obviously you can see why that happens from all the pushing and breathing.

Moving on with the story, even with all this pushing that was going on, it's hard to see any forward progress happening. We tried many different pushing positions to try to get the labor moving. Some women have back labor which is a major pain in your back caused by your baby's position against your pelvis. Some of my friends had this and they said it was extremely uncomfortable and painful. I didn't have back labor, but I felt like I was going to be there for days, and God was torturing me. I knew it, he was torturing me for having sex!

Finally, the doctor told me I only had a few more pushes left. They said the baby was "crowning," which is when they can start to see the head coming out of your vagina.

They asked if I wanted to put a mirror down there to see what was happening and I looked at them like they were crazy… um, I'll pass on this one too. Crowning was a bit uncomfortable and exactly what you think it would feel like. Something is trying to escape your vagina, but your vagina isn't big enough. It's a weird sensation once you have an epidural because you could technically feel the pressure of the baby's head coming out, but you couldn't feel your legs or feet at all. If you don't end up getting an epidural, there's this thing called "the ring of fire" where if you are giving birth vaginally and the baby starts coming out, it pushes on and stretches your vaginal opening causing a burning stinging sensation. Ouch!

My husband is a firefighter, so it was always in the plan for him to deliver our babies and cut the umbilical cord. The umbilical cord is a tube that connects you to your baby during pregnancy and carries food and oxygen from the placenta to your baby. It also has two arteries that carry waste from your baby back to the placenta. It can be up to 22 inches long.

One last push and my husband caught/pulled the baby out, and they put him on my chest. Luckily one of my friends told me to expect the baby was going to be gray so I wouldn't freak out when they put him on top of me. Sure enough, the baby looked like a little alien, gray, covered in blood, and slimy (oh, and they might poop on you).

But he also came out and wasn't crying. In every single movie when a baby is delivered, it's always crying. So, I panicked and asked the nurses if he was ok, and why wasn't he crying? They all sort of laughed at me and told me that was normal.

They let the baby lay on my chest for a while for "bonding time" and then they take them, clean them up, weigh them, measure, and swaddle them up in a blanket. They gave the baby to my husband while they cleaned me up—and by cleaned me up, I mean pushed hard on my stomach to ensure the placenta and all the blood came out also.

The placenta is an organ that develops in your uterus during pregnancy. It provides oxygen and nutrients to your growing baby and removes waste products from your baby's blood. The nurse was so excited when she got it out of me and wanted to show me. She wanted me to look at or hold this dark colored bloody blob. I took one look and I said, "Nope, no thank you." But she made me look and told me it looked like the tree of life, literally giving the baby life inside of me and that it was such a beautiful thing.

I wasn't convinced, and it still looked like a deflated large brown Whoopee cushion with veins on it. I found out later that some people encapsulate it and take them as pills after. Placenta encapsulation is the act of steaming, dehydrating, and crushing placenta, then putting the resulting powder into pills or capsules for consumption. This consumption is usually done by a mother after childbirth and is believed to have some health benefits, though that is not medically proven. Pretty disgusting if you ask me.

There is also something unique that can come from the umbilical cord blood. Stem cells can be gathered from the umbilical cord and saved in the case that your child has cancer later in life and the cord blood can be used to treat over 80 other life-threatening diseases. The body is pretty darn cool.

They moved me to the bathroom to try to make sure I could pee after taking the catheter out. Oh yeah, forgot to mention they use a catheter on you, so you don't pee on the bed. I don't even remember them putting it in or taking it out because of the epidural but, who knew! It was so hard to walk to the bathroom because everything was still numb, but that angel of a nurse was with me and literally wiped me all up and walked me back to the bed. I had no idea how much blood you lose during childbirth. Women usually lose about half a quart during vaginal birth or about 1 quart after a c-section birth.

A C-section is a major abdominal surgery where they cut through the skin, fat, fascia, muscle, peritoneum, uterus, and amniotic sac to be able to pull the baby out.

When I came back to the bed, it literally looked like a scene from the show Dexter. Blood and guts were everywhere.

Now, of course, this was the most eventful birth story for me but for my second baby, it was a breeze. We went in at 11:00PM and had the baby that morning. I pushed for forty minutes, and it was over. Sometimes you win and sometimes you lose.

I remember telling the nurse, "Oh my gosh, I'm so happy that thing is out of me, and I feel ten pounds lighter!"

She laughed and told me, "You are!"

"Everyone expects you to be nothing less than overjoyed. But the reality is many women end up in a dark, discouraging place and don't know where to turn or who to ask about it. We are supposed to be 100% grateful and over the moon. We have been blessed with motherhood when many women never get the honor, so guilt clouds us when we feel depressed, hopeless, utterly exhausted, and barely hanging on.
It's not talked about enough.

It needs to be."
~Unknown

CHAPTER 7

Congratulations it's a....

I was exhausted and relieved. I wanted to see the baby but didn't really want to hold him, and preferred my husband to watch him. But they gave him to me anyway to feed because he was probably hungry. Not only are you exhausted and want to be done, but now the real work and pain begins, feeding the baby every two hours for the rest of your life.

Just kidding on the rest of your life part, but feeding the baby constantly was something I was not prepared for.

After we got cleaned up, they put me in a wheelchair holding the baby and they took us to yet another private room. I immediately put on a postpartum sculpting girdle so that it would help my abs tighten back up quicker and with less pain. I highly recommend this, so it doesn't feel like your guts are falling out of your stomach every time you take a step.

Not knowing what the heck I was doing; they had a different nurse come in and help with breast-feeding. She showed me how to breastfeed and made sure my son had a good latch on my breast. She explained my milk would be coming in soon but this early, only what they call colostrum was coming out. Colostrum is extremely important for the baby after birth because it has all the right nutrients. I was confused, stuff was coming out of my boobs, but it wasn't milk?

After a bit I explained to her that it was super painful and she considered if the baby had a tongue-tie, which is when they'd need to loosen the bottom of the baby's tongue with a small cut to make sure they can suck correctly and get fed. But then she thought maybe it was just a bad latch or because my nipples are inverted, which can be painful when the baby pulls the nipple outright. She suggested a nipple shield, which is like a plastic bottle nipple that goes over your nipple and helps the baby start sucking. But that didn't seem to work at all.

I didn't know what I was doing, but I did know it probably wasn't supposed to hurt that bad. It felt like Edward Scissorhands were grabbing my boob and cutting it with a million pieces of glass. More to come on this later but let's just say breast-feeding was not any fun from beginning to end, but again this was my story.

We were so happy that the hard part was over. We shared the good news with family and friends and slowly, but surely, everyone started showing up. Of course, this was pre-Covid time, and we had as many as ten people in the room with us at one time passing the baby around, waiting for their chance to hold him.

We were lucky that although I didn't have the best experience, we got to hold the baby and care for it right away. In some cases, that's not possible. If there are major complications with the birth, the baby could go directly to the NICU which is the Neonatal Intensive Care Unit. Most babies admitted to the NICU are born preterm most likely before 37 weeks of pregnancy, they have low birth weight under 5 pounds or have a health condition.

The NICU provides around-the-clock care from a team of experts. This can be extremely difficult because sometimes you may or may not be able to hold your baby. Parents can spend time with them, but they're most likely put into what's called an incubator that keeps the baby safe from the external environment. They are used in combination with other equipment and procedures to ensure babies are safe and can grow and become healthy quicker. Other family members may or may not be able to visit the baby as well. I can't imagine what this would do to one's psyche directly after birth. I think those parents who have to have a child in the NICU are so strong and brave.

Since we were able to care for the baby right away, there were so many opinions going around, and like with any family, tension in the room. Little did I know that this was when my postpartum anxiety would begin. Was someone going to get mad that someone else was holding him too long? Who was going to show up to see the baby? Who wasn't going to show up to see the baby? Was someone going to say something inappropriate? Was someone going to steal the baby? Is everyone judging me? Are my friends going to show up? Did I still even have friends? Who am I now? Can anyone tell I'm freaking out? So many questions in my head. So much anxiety.

Also at this time, so many different people were coming in and out of the room. We had a person come in to take pictures for us if we wanted them to—and it only cost $150 dollars! We didn't get swindled the second time, believe me. We had people coming in for hospital paperwork, and for the baby's social security and name. We had people coming in and taking the baby's blood, doing hearing tests, exams, showing us how to bathe the baby, breast-feeding consultants, nurses checking on me…it was all sort of a blur.

I remember the feeling, while filling out the paperwork for the baby's name, that it all seemed so permanent. Up until that point, I knew I was having a baby and had accepted it, but it never really hit me that I'd be responsible for this child for the rest of my life. I mean legally until they're 18, but, realistically, the rest of my life. I shrugged it off until that pen hit the paper and the ink was dry. I picked the name this child would have for the rest of their life. I was responsible for how they will be defined and how the world will see them until they can choose to do that themselves. It's such a weird feeling to have all this responsibility and feeling like you have no qualifications.

The one thing I remember is the hospital staff asking us if we wanted to have the baby circumcised. Most boys have skin that completely covers, or almost covers, the end of the penis. Circumcision removes some of this foreskin so that the tip of the penis is exposed to air. Circumcision has pros and cons and has been a religious rite for thousands of years. There are certain medical benefits like lower risk of urinary tract infections, protection from penile cancer, and certain sexually transmitted diseases.

We knew we did want the circumcision, so they had to take the baby to another room because it was a surgical procedure and I got so worried they were going to switch the baby with someone else's baby. I asked if they had to and if we could go and they said no, so I had to put my trust in them. They do have matching bracelets for the baby and mom to make sure this doesn't happen but still…come on, I know I'm not the only one who watches the crazy lifetime movies where people steal and switch babies.

My dad asked me if I wanted anything to eat and I told him a footlong sandwich from Subway because now I could eat deli meat (remember?)! Hooray! I ate that thing so freaking fast. It was so good, and I was so appreciative of him for not forgetting about me. After all the visitors left, it was just my husband, me, and my little baby boy.

I can't understand how nobody prepares you for what is next after you have a baby. Good luck, you did good! That's all you get.

You know, in other cultures they have more support than we have in the United States. Some women have to go back to work after two weeks.

The Chinese tradition for new mothers and their babies is called zuo yue zi or "sitting month" where they receive full-time care at a private postnatal center. A new mother stays indoors for one month and refrains from all activities. They have full on postpartum hotels for this. Can you imagine?

The Latin American tradition has something similar, with a forty-day recovery period to bond with the baby avoiding housework, exercise, and sex and the taking of herbal baths.

The Korean tradition is a 21-day postpartum care period called Saam-chil-il. You can hire a specialist to perform special massages, take care of household chores and cook for you.

The Mexican tradition is known as la cuarentena. They avoid cold showers, drink hot soups, abstain from sex, and bind the abdomen with a postpartum belt.

The Muslim tradition is a 40-day rest period.

In Spain, you can receive a cartilla de embarazo (Mother's passport) and have a midwife check in monthly.

For African or West Indies traditions, they massage their stomach with hot water, take a sitz bath—which is a really hot bath—drink hot water, limit their outings with the baby for a minimum of one month

Japanese, Malay, Eastern Indian Hindus, and South African women also have a period of rest.

In Finland, mothers can apply at 22 weeks pregnant for a free box through the social security system that has around 63 essential items for the baby and the box can double as a bed for the baby.

In Australia they don't allow your partner stay overnight with you, unless it's a private suite, so it's just you and your baby to bond. Eligible employees who are the main caregiver for the baby can get up to 18 weeks paid parental leave paid at the national minimum wage. Can you imagine over 4 months of paid leave?!

The Native American Shoshone tribe requires the new mother to live alone with her baby for the first month to foster a bond between the two.

In contrast some Native American mothers would return to their usual duties very quickly, according to the National History Education Clearinghouse. To allow new mothers to resume their duties, babies were swaddled and strapped to a cradleboard, which was carried on the mother's back and in more modern society they use a baby sling.

There are lots of ways that we can connect with our baby and rest, but the main point of all of this is that rest is essential for mothers. Recovery is important. We don't have to do it all the second the baby comes into this world. We may not have such a luxury in the United States for a rest period but luckily, we had great nurses who showed us how to bathe the baby, swaddle the baby, change the diaper, take care of the belly button and privates we just had circumcised. Our family supported us as much as they could but there were no videos, books, or resources to prepare us for what was coming next. But don't forget, there are many resources out there like home visitors that could help if you do your research!

There are certain ways to get help if you can't afford diapers as well. Check your local nonprofit providers for any diaper banks. I was part of the Junior League that had a diaper bank that had thousands of diapers that they fundraise for and then provide to organizations to supply to parents in need. If you don't have enough, you can find opportunities that can assist.

We stayed in the hospital overnight to ensure the baby and I were doing well. A nurse came in occasionally, and in the middle of the night to check on me and the baby. I couldn't sleep the entire first night for either baby. The whole night I was worried he was going to stop breathing, both for selfish reasons of not wanting to go through it all again, and for the sake of the baby. I would just sit there watching them sleep, the baby and my husband, questioning everything. It wasn't until the nurse came in the next morning that she told me it was normal for the baby to sleep the entire first night. I didn't realize the baby was just as exhausted. Too little too late but at least I can share with you now.

The hospital staff discharged us quickly and I remember getting ready to go home and getting more nervous as the time went by. I don't know why I didn't realize or expect it, but when the bill came for the labor and delivery, I was shocked. According to data collected by Fair Health, the average cost of having a vaginal delivery is between $5,000 and $11,000 in most states. The numbers are higher for C-sections, with prices ranging from $7,500 to $14,500.

The first time my husband left the hospital room to go get the car—and I don't know why because I'd always been so confident with other people's kids when I baby-sat—I felt so alone, scared, and unsure.

Who decided to trust us with this baby?

Who signed off that we were going to be good parents?

They hospital staff got me in a wheelchair and took us down to the car that my husband had brought around to the front of the hospital. I sat in the back with the baby and remembered every little bump on the ride home, feeling like we were going to get in an accident and something terrible was going to happen to the baby. I was sure of it. I wish someone would have talked to us about postpartum, what the signs were, and what to look out for. I wish we would've known about meal trains, where your friends and family sign up to bring you meals the first few weeks after you get home. Some people did bring food when they visited but mostly, they just wanted to see the baby. Even though you may be seeing a lot of people, this is the time where I felt very unseen and ignored that I had given birth. People would walk in straight to the baby and completely ignore me. Now thinking back on how I felt, imagine how my husband felt!

This began my 4th trimester, as they call it after the baby is born. Rougher than the 3rd for me, and I literally couldn't have made it through without my husband, my literal rock holding me up through the most challenging time I ever would have imagined.

For both pregnancies, from the time I found out I was pregnant until after labor, I never felt like the baby was mine. I told people I was raising my husband's baby because it just didn't feel like I owned it, or like it came out of me. I felt more like God gave it to me. I unintentionally called him an "it" for the longest time. I had nearly zero connection with the baby and to top it all off, he came out with blonde hair and blue eyes.

For context, my husband and I both have brown hair and brown eyes. Nobody told me that your family's genetics can be inherited by your baby, and they could look nothing like you.

So not only did I not feel an emotional connection to him, but it also felt as though I didn't have a physical one either.

You know, the common questions and comments people get when they're pregnant are, "Aren't you so excited?" "He's going to be so cute." "Do you like when he kicks?" "Aren't you happy it's a boy?" "This is going to be the best time of your life."

But I never once felt true happiness or excitement from having this baby. I wasn't very shy about it either. I also didn't feel apologetic about that because they were my true feelings.

Even though it made a lot of people feel awkward, I'd always give honest answers to their questions. From the moment I was pregnant, I felt like my life was going to be over. Co-workers would call me, "mama" and I would get so upset. I remember the first time this happened, I was stunned and tried to ignore it. One time an older male called me "mama" and I immediately responded, "Please don't call me that. I don't walk around calling you 'daddy' if you have kids." After a few times of expecting and anticipating this from random people I barely talked to, or even close acquaintances, I responded and told them:

"Don't call me mama, my name is Mariah."

This was me, hanging on by a thread of who I was, and trying not to let this thing that was happening to me define me. I felt singled out and as though everyone was looking at me like I had a piece of lettuce in my teeth. Like they could see inside my soul and know I was pregnant.

It's a lot to deal with all these emotional changes, not to mention the physical changes that happen. My hair started to fall out in clumps, and then once it falls out, you begin to pop up with baby hairs in the front of your hair line. I didn't know this could happen! Your boobs start getting bigger from all the milk and you get stretch marks everywhere. I got stretch marks on my stomach, my breasts, and my legs.

I honestly didn't even know what they were at first because they come in like a whitish color and then turn to a deeper red/purple color. And they itch. No matter how much lotion or product you put on them to help, they still grow, and they still itch. Just like pregnancy, for as much as you may want it to stop hurting, your stomach just keeps growing and you keep getting bigger and bigger. You can wear belly bands to help with putting your insides back together. They make belly wraps for both your waist and hips. These bands help your posture and alignment while supporting your uterus while it returns to its normal size. It basically helps your muscles remember what to do after the baby comes out. I was not prepared to still look pregnant months after having the baby, even with a belly wrap.

Birth is not only
about making babies.
It's about making
mothers;
STRONG,
COMPETENT,
CAPABLE MOTHERS
who trust themselves
and believe in their
inner strength."
~Barbara Katz Rothman

CHAPTER 8

Bringing home the bacon and the milk

PUMPING IN A VACANT OFFICE AT WORK I LOOK HAPPY BUT INSIDE I FELT ISOLATED AND INFURIATED THAT I HAD TO PUT MY BODY THROUGH MORE PAIN.

Nothing, and I mean nothing, could have prepared me for what was coming next. From the day we got home from the hospital to about a year later, was a blur to me. It was the hardest year of my life. Everyone told me that breast-feeding was going to be so special and that it would begin to create a unique bond between the baby and I. But something happened to me when I was breast-feeding, or rather, trying to breastfeed.

I had so many questions that would go unanswered.

Was I feeding him enough? Was he gaining enough weight? Was it normal for it to be hurting so much? Why was I crying when I was feeding him? Why did my boobs hurt this bad? Was I producing enough? Did my milk come in? How long did I have to do this? Did I even have to do this? Can't my husband do this? Why the hell did Eve have to bite that apple?

The baby would start crying and babies only cry for a few reasons at the newborn age, either they are hungry, dirty, or tired and it always seemed to be that the baby was hungry. This began to trigger a deep feeling inside, like an internal doom I couldn't really express, because every time I even mentioned something close to being unhappy while breast-feeding, people would look at me like I was crazy and overreacting or I was doing it wrong. Everyone except my husband.

I could truly feel his empathy for me every time the baby cried. He'd tell me, "I would if I could," but then still hand me the baby to feed. I'd let the baby latch and instantly feel the pain on my nipple. And then as I'm trying to breathe through that pain, a second wave of pain would start to tingle in the depths of my abdomen and breasts.

This second wave was something they called "let down." It generally feels a bit uncomfortable for the milk to let down, but I felt physical pain. I didn't know it at the time, and I wasn't technically diagnosed but after doing research of my own, I found there's a condition called Dysmorphic Milk Ejection Reflex (D-MER). The official definition for D-MER is a condition where women who breastfeed develop negative emotions that begin just before the milk ejection reflex and last less than a few minutes. It is different from postpartum depression, breast-feeding aversion, and agitation (BAA), or a dislike of breast-feeding.

The actual feeling for me is hard to put in words, but it was very close to that feeling right before a panic attack. I couldn't breathe, and I felt like I was losing control and spinning farther away from reality. And I wanted to cry my eyes out for no reason. I felt that every time I breast fed, which is basically a million times. To top it all off, there's this thing that happens with mothers that if you hear a baby crying you start to let down because that is your body's natural reaction to need to care for a child. Literally any baby, not just your own baby. Be prepared when you are in public for this because it's not very fun.

There is so much pressure put on a pregnant woman to breastfeed. From the time you come into the doctor for your first checkup, to the time you are feeding your baby for the first time after delivery, everyone is pushing breast-feeding versus formula. They have breast-feeding consultants come and talk with you and if you have concerns about anything. They try and persuade you to stick with it because it's the best for the baby, best for bonding, best nutrition, just best overall choice. Breastfed is best.

For the first baby, I only made it to ten months. I was torn between the health of the baby and my own mental health when considering if I wanted to continue breast-feeding past the ten months or not.

The second baby, I was prepared. I knew what it was going to feel like and still the doctors and nurses would try to persuade me to breast-feeding. I told my husband I would try my best, but I was not going to put my health, either physically or mentally, in jeopardy again. I tried again with my second, hopeful that it would be different, but it was so painful, the same teeth gritting, nail biting pain I had with the first child. I lasted a week. After a week, I chose to pump the remainder of the first year to give my baby the breast milk and had zero regrets.

The one thing that I cannot go without talking about is leaking from your breasts. Leaking all the time. Leaking every time, you take your bra off, in the shower, through your shirts, during sex, taking a bath, when you hear a baby cry or even think about your baby (yes, this is real). Before we had the baby, my husband was insistent that we buy burp rags. I didn't know why he wanted so many freaking rags, I mean we literally had like forty. But let me tell you, boy did these rags come in handy when I was breast-feeding! Between the baby spitting up, leaking out the side of his mouth when he would eat, or just to clean myself up after a feeding.

I researched so much information about having a baby, went to all the pre-baby classes, and thought I was set. But I still didn't realize how many breast-feeding pads I would go through because I'd be leaking all the time. It's important to clean yourself up really good after you feed because you could get an infection. Literally after every single time I slathered myself with nipple cream so that it would ease the pain and provide moisture to your nipples to help prevent bleeding, cracking, or itching during breast-feeding. I started with this cheap hand-me-down, then turned to disposables, and realized quickly I needed more high-quality fabric I could rely on.

For me, I really liked Bamboobies. These were the softest things I had ever felt, and they were reusable so I could use a ton and just wash them at the end of the week and not worry about it. Let me tell you, these were lifesavers. They have day pads which are heart-shaped and not as thick, and night pads which are super absorbent and really do last all night. For those that may not be able to afford these, I would reach out to your local non-profits to see what supplies they may have for this.

I also didn't realize it was a thing to overproduce milk. I had heard a few stories of people not being able to produce enough and how frustrating that was. People can eat certain cookies and drink certain tea to help produce, but overproducing? Who knew that could even happen? One of the first few days we were home, I had been feeding the baby every two hours because when they are that little, they can feed that frequently. Suddenly I started to feel one of my boobs get really hard and hurt.

I didn't realize it at the time, but my mom recognized it right away and said I was engorged. This is when you don't ensure your boobs are empty after a feeding and it just builds up as you continue to produce milk. She told me to take a hot shower and massage the milk out before, or I'd get a clogged duct in my breast. Oh yeah, clogged ducts are a thing and one of the best ways to get it unclogged from research, and experience, was to use a vibrator.

Yes, I said it. It has another use. And thank goodness for this because having a clogged duct and not taking care of it correctly quickly turns into this amazing, unforgettable experience called Mastitis. Mastitis is an inflammation of breast tissue that sometimes involves an infection. The inflammation results in breast pain, swelling, warmth and redness. You might also have fever and chills. I didn't realize I had this at the time, but it was, yet again, another excruciating pain that took a few days of massaging and antibiotics to get rid of. A cause of mastitis can be what's called "blebs" which is a tiny milk blister on the nipple or areola that restricts milk flow, therefore causing mastitis. They tend to usually resolve themselves within 48 hours but can last weeks at a time. Let your doctor know if you think you have one.

Back to the engorgement. I got in the shower and massaged as hard as I could with a hot rag to release the milk. My nipples were so sensitive from being constantly pulled on that the water from the shower stung like antiseptic on an open wound. I literally couldn't take a shower without putting a washcloth over my nipples the entire time so the water wouldn't hit them at all.

So, turns out I was an over-producer of milk as well. My baby literally wouldn't drink all of the milk each feeding, so I'd have to stand over the sink massaging the milk out of my boob after every feeding. Finally, I got smart and started pumping afterward, to make sure they were empty and then I had that milk to store.

I highly recommend you try to save every ounce of milk you produce, or the baby doesn't eat. This will lessen the time you will need to breastfeed if it's uncomfortable like it was for me. I over-produced so much we ended up buying a second freezer. By the time I couldn't breastfeed any longer because of the mental and physical pain, we had up to eight months' worth of frozen milk in our freezer! It was important for me to try to do this because of the benefits of breastmilk, it contains white blood cells and antibodies to fight infections, it has hydration and nutrition our baby needs, it lowers baby's risk of common illnesses, it's a natural pain reliever, and it's constantly changing to meet your baby's needs. You can also give it to your others kids when they are sick to help with antibodies. It's also important to know there are specific guidelines of storing milk depending on the time you pumped and the storage location temperature. You want to be careful you follow this, so you don't give your baby spoiled milk.

Breast milk is an amazing thing that can be used in many ways. Some studies have shown that women can store anywhere from 2.5oz to 5oz in each breast. I was pumping 20 ounces each time. Each time you feed the baby from your breast, that is a signal to your body that it needs to start producing more. The longer the milk sits in your breast without being emptied, that sends a signal to your body that it doesn't need to produce as much milk. When you do overproduce, or the baby doesn't drink the entire bottle you can save the excess milk for up to a full year in the freezer. You can mix it with solid food when the baby is ready. You can pour a little in your baby's bath to lock in moisture and prevent dryness.

Overproducing is also hard for the baby because when they go to latch, it's like trying to drink from a fire hose. I learned that I would let the baby suck until the milk let down, then I'd let the rush pass, and when I say pass, I mean squirt out like a sprinkler, until it was barely dripping, and then I'd put the baby back on to my breast to drink. This would help me deal with the pain from D-Mer as well, allowing me to get through it by breathing deeply and then deal with the normal pain of having the baby fed separately.

As I said before, for the first pregnancy, I breastfed for ten months. This was very hard because I didn't think there was another choice. I'd breastfeed at home, go to work and pump, and breastfeed again when I got back. It wasn't until my second pregnancy that I made the choice early on to breastfeed as long as I could, and then pump the rest of the time. And boy, did I not care one bit because I knew how much time, sadness, pain, and anxiety I was saving myself and my family.

It's important to know that pain during breast-feeding—outside the first month, maybe six weeks—is not normal. I haven't ever personally talked with someone with as much pain as I had the duration of breast-feeding. I want to be sure you know that if something doesn't feel right speak up.

Please speak up no matter what people are telling you.

This goes for everything throughout your pregnancy, after your pregnancy, and even if it's years after. I have learned in motherhood, that you are not in control of much other than your instincts, and if you lose those, you might lose yourself. That is one of the things I take pride in after having kids. Speaking up for myself when I knew something wasn't right. You are your own advocate. Whether it was trying to get my third epidural right, getting numbing nipple balm cream from a pharmacy (who knew this even existed), or getting help for postpartum depression, I've always taken pride in my decisions to stand up for myself (or others) when something didn't seem right.

Another helpful tip: something that really helped me through breast-feeding was getting an App on your phone for tracking feedings, diaper changing, and stretches of sleep. Because I was an overproducer, I'd time my feedings to ensure I was even on both sides. I'd put the baby on one side, start the "Right" timer, switch sides, and start the "Left" timer. This helped me keep track of, not only the time of feedings, but how long each feeding lasted. There are certain guides out there that help you ensure the baby is getting enough milk. The average time you should be feeding or pumping is around twenty minutes on each side. Because I was an overproducer, I pumped around ten minutes on each side. There's also breast-feeding groups you can attend that weigh the baby before and after a feeding to see how much milk they are getting. But I trusted the baby to eat as much as he needed and tried not to worry about that other stuff.

Another thing that was super helpful was having multiple breast pumps. Usually, the first breast pump is covered by insurance and any additional ones are out of pocket. I found my second pump at a yard sale. I finally weaned myself from feeding every two hours, to every four hours and then eight at night. This is where I slowly prolonged the time between feedings so that my body would get the signal I didn't need to produce as much and as often. It's important to know how to use a pump correctly otherwise this will cause you pain. It took a few weeks to regulate my body and get on a schedule.

Making sure you have the right flange size affects how your body reacts to pumping and ensures you produce the most breast milk in the least amount of time. Like, literally get a ruler out and measure your nipple. I bought two different sizes to see which would work and sent the other back. I ended up getting a larger one that I needed and had to use nipple balm every time I pumped to help with the rubbing. Ensuring this will also ensure you don't get clogged ducts, pain, and decreased milk.

Weaning is a whole process that you must be very careful with as well, so that your breasts don't get engorged or clogged. But having cabbage on hand and putting that over your breasts will help dry up your breast milk or help when you are engorged. Isn't that such a silly thing to think about? Throwing some random food on your breasts like we are back to Adam and Eve days will seriously save you some pain. Slowly but surely, is the best way.

Having two pumps was so nice. I would keep one at home and one at work, that way I would not have to lug it around or clean it after every use. Cleaning the pump parts is extremely important because bacteria can grow fast from the breastmilk. It's okay not to wash them right away after use, but be sure to disinfect them again before using because it could cause bacteria to get into the breast milk or your breast. Because of this, I bought extra parts and then boiled them all together once every other day to make sure the parts were disinfected.

They also have special microwave bags you can use right after you pump that disinfect them also. This was huge in a time crunch. Lugging the pump around was a pain because it's not only the pump, but the pump connections, pump parts, bottles, caps, bags, pads, extra bras, extra shirts, etc. I bought my own diaper bag just to keep all my pump parts in. I also bought a car charger connection for it because you never know when you'll get stuck in the car on your way home from work, not having had the chance to pump the last half of the day, and you're leaking all over, and just need to let it out!

One last thing—and something my husband was super helpful with—was keeping me fed. I know it sounds silly, but after you have the baby and start producing milk, you are hungry all the time. But at the same time, you don't really have space to feel anything at all. So, self-care can go out the window. There were times when my husband would literally take the baby from me, and tell me to go eat, or he'd put food in front of me to make sure I'd eat. If you don't then, not only will you lose energy, but your milk supply will suffer. If I'd skip a meal, I'd produce only half the milk I did before. So, if you don't have that support, I would try to food prep as much as possible so you can just warm something up quickly in the microwave or eat a protein bar, fruit, snacks, anything at this point. Make sure you are fully hydrated and fully fed.

Public breast-feeding. No one prepared me to be half-naked in front of not only my family, but my in-laws. I was prepared to feed the baby in front of my husband because, obviously, he's seen all of me, but when the baby would start crying, everyone would just stare at me until I started feeding them. Every time it felt as though they all stopped what they were doing and waited till I pulled my boob out to feed. It was so awkward and uncomfortable. Eventually I bought a breast-feeding scarf to cover up in public. I am all for female empowerment and not feeling the need to cover up, but for me, it really helped me relax, especially in public. The scarves are really cool and literally a fashion scarf but it's long and wide enough to wrap around your side and cover the baby while you feed if you want a little privacy.

During this time, I continued to be surrounded by people full of joy for my new baby but I honestly, still felt so alone. My mental health was suffering.

"The emotional labor pains
of becoming a mother are
far greater than the
physical pangs of birth;
these are the growing
surges of your heart as it
pushes out selfishness and
fear and makes room for
sacrifice and love. It is a
private and silent birth of
the soul, but it is no less
holy than the event of
childbirth—perhaps even
more sacred."
~Joy Kusek

CHAPTER 9

I'm fine, it's fine
Everything is fine

CRYING WHILE I WAS BREAST-FEEDING WITH PAIN, TRYING TO SAVE MILK ON THE OTHER BREAST WITH MY HAAKAA PUMP AND TRYING TO SHOW MY SON SOME LOVE.

Breast-feeding was only the start of my postpartum journey. I've heard it called the 4th trimester which makes sense because your body doesn't stop changing just after the 3rd trimester.

The 4th trimester is considered the first 12 weeks after the baby is born, where physical and emotional changes continue to happen.

When my husband and I first arrived home with our new baby, we put the car seat down, put our bags down, and looked at each other's faces with panic, like, "Now what?" I didn't realize that we'd need to set up an appointment with the pediatrician three days after having the baby. Which doesn't make any sense to me why we have to see the pediatrician before we get checked out by our Obstetrician (OB) doctor. They gave us a list of pediatricians in the hospital, and we were like really…? We just choose one?

Thankfully, the nurse gave us a few recommendations and we have a wonderful pediatrician now, but it would be nice if there'd been a little more information on the lists—which were in our area, how long they'd been in practice, were they male or female? The generic list was not very helpful. I suggest you do your own research beforehand because after the baby comes, you don't have mental capacity to think of things like that. You are literally on overload.

Eventually, we got into the swing of things with the baby, figuring out a schedule of our own. I was lucky that my husband was able to take time off of work for six weeks to help me. I honestly would have probably lost my mind if he wasn't able to do this. The daytime was pretty doable; we'd wake up, feed and change the baby, play with the baby, and then put them down for a nap. I'd eat right after feeding the baby, or when the baby was napping, because I'd have to feed right upon waking. My mom would always tell me, sleep when the baby sleeps!

The nighttime, however, was rough and unexpected. Nobody told me that the baby wakes depending on when it gets hungry. This could be every two hours, or it could be every four to six hours. It's not predictable, at least not for a while. There's a meme I often see that says, my husband and I share the load of the baby, he sleeps because I can't, and I feed because he can't. This is totally true. In the middle of the night, when the baby wakes up, it's impossible not to feel jealous or frustrated with your significant other because, even if they wanted to help, they can't, because when you're breast-feeding, you are literally the only thing that can feed your baby.

Some two weeks after I got home, collapsing from emotional and physical exhaustion, I woke up and the room was spinning.

I rarely drink alcohol, and there was only one time I overdid it and got drunk, dizzy, throwing up everywhere (those were the days I should've taken more advantage of, but that's neither here nor there). But this felt similar. I heard the baby cry and woke up to feed him in the early morning when the sun wasn't even out yet. As I stood and stepped from my bed, I felt completely off. I ran to the bathroom and tried to throw up, thinking maybe I had food poisoning or a virus or something.

I remember sitting in the bathroom and everything was spinning. It didn't seem to matter if my eyes were open or closed, I felt like I was stuck inside a washer and everything around me was spinning and the clothes whirling around me.

I endured this for about two weeks, trying every medication we could find recommended for dizziness. I tried going to a homeopathic healer that worked on my jaw/ear. I even tried ear candles; I mean literally anything I could try to stop the dizziness, I tried. It got so bad that I'd have to lay down most of the day with my eyes closed. I couldn't really move or do much because everything made it worse. At night I'd wake up when the baby would, and my angel of a husband would have to get up, get the baby, bring the baby to me in bed where I'd feed him, and hand him back to my husband. I dreaded going to the bathroom because it felt a mile away and I just couldn't make the trip without insane dizziness.

All I remember feeling at the time was the dread that this would never go away. I feared what would happen if it didn't pass. On top of barely being present, I wouldn't even be able to work because I work on a computer. I don't remember how many times I prayed or spent time talking to God during this time, but it felt like He was nowhere to be seen. It felt like He wasn't listening, and I couldn't understand why. Why was He letting this happen to me? Why wasn't He listening? Why didn't He just fix it so I could just take care of my baby?

Eventually, I got to the point where I couldn't handle the dizziness.

After about two weeks of constantly throwing up and doing nothing but sleeping, I was sitting in the bathroom and called for my husband. I told him I thought something was very wrong. At first, he'd thought the same thing as me, that I either ate something or just had a weird virus, but he supported me to go to the hospital.

I called my mom to come and get me and take me to the emergency room, because, at this point, I couldn't go more than a couple of hours without throwing up or at least dry heaving what was left in my stomach. My husband was a Godsend and stepped up so much to care for us that, by this point, we had some breast milk in the freezer for back-up.

I remember sitting in the E.R., in the gross, overcrowded waiting room with my mom, for what seemed like an eternity. I had to sit with a vomit-bag in case I was going to throw up again. Finally, I got to a room and waited for the doctor. By this time, I think it was the longest I'd gone without pumping or feeding, and my boobs felt like rocks. You could literally poke them and there was no give at all. Of course, the E.R. doesn't have a breast-pump, so I had to hand massage the milk out. But I didn't want to waste it, so I sat there on the hospital bed, massaging my boob-milk into the urine collection test cup while my mom looked at me laughing like I was crazy.

I mean seriously, who does this?

A crazy breast-feeding mom who doesn't want to waste a drop, that's who. I felt that I was physically and mentally losing it.

Finally, they took me back and told me I had something called Vertigo. Vertigo is a symptom, rather than a condition where you feel a sudden internal or external spinning sensation caused by a change in the inner ear. I had no idea what it was before this. They gave me an I.V. and some medicine, and I went home.

I was torn between relief and happiness because they actually said something was wrong with me, and fear and dread because there really isn't a cure for vertigo. You basically just have to deal with it until your brain adjusts, or it stops.

Although we never did find the cause of it, I have come to suspect that this was a rare side-effect of the anesthesiologist giving me three different epidurals, two of which were in the wrong part of my back.

Throughout this entire time after I got over vertigo, my family was checking in on me, calling and texting, but it was hard to deal with because everyone just wanted to see the baby. When they'd come over, they'd say "How are you?" or "Are you any better?" but then go straight to the baby to "help." But truthfully, it was more stressful than helpful, because everyone seemed to gloss over me and my husband, and it felt like they really didn't care how we were. They just wanted to hold the baby.

Look, I get it, they thought they were helping. But it made things worse for me because I then had to stop resting, sit up, have a conversation, and feel like I had to entertain while internally I was screaming. It got to the point where we had multiple family members over at a time, and our house was like a revolving door from morning to night.

We have a ton of family, and I'm extremely grateful for them. I don't know what I would do without both of our families helping as we raise our kids. But during that first week, I couldn't handle it.

We learned from this the second time around.

We told everyone we weren't having visitors for the first week, that we needed our time to adjust, find our schedule, and just relax for a second before everyone bombarded us. We were nervous to enforce the new boundaries, but we knew we had to do it to save our mental health.

And guess what, everyone understood, and not one person complained. Before having kids, the only boundary I knew was the three-point boundary on a basketball court. This is extremely important to know your limits and boundaries of what is okay and what is not ok, especially concerning your kids. It's also important to not feel guilty by enforcing them. This will save you mentally and physically. It is impossible to please everyone, but it is very possible to please yourself.

"A GIRL SHOULD BE TWO THINGS:

Who & What She Wants"

~Coco Chanel

CHAPTER 10

There's a First Time for Everything

There are lots of firsts that you will go through after having a baby and I'm going to talk about a few that blew my mind.

First Poop:

The nurse told me to make sure I took some sort of stool softener because apparently your first poop after labor is a doozie (pun intended). Certain medications like antihistamines can make it harder to go as well. It's important to stay hydrated during this time so that you are not in pain when you have to go.

First Shower:

I didn't want to shower at the hospital because their showers always seemed so dirty and we were only there a day, so when we got home, the first thing I did was strip and get in the shower. I remember the water hitting me all over and feeling relief. I felt free of the baby, free of the pain, free of all the ooey gooey blood coming out of me all over the shower floor like I just killed someone. Once all the blood was cleared up, my breasts started leaking. And this didn't bother me too much in the shower but the second you step out it's like your internal sprinkler doesn't have a shut off valve.

First Pee:

This wasn't too bad for me either because my vagina didn't tear, and I didn't have an episiotomy during labor. An episiotomy is a surgical cut made at the opening of the vagina during childbirth, to aid a difficult delivery and prevent the rupture of tissues.

Let me make one correction. I was told I didn't have a tear, but when I sat down to pee it burned like I had a U.T.I. They give you this little water bottle to fill up with warm water and squirt on your vagina while you pee so that it eases the pain a bit. This is so awkward but thank God for that little water bottle because, for sure it did ease the pain. I think I used that for the first few days because I did end up having a tiny tear that needed to heal more. Apparently, there are these cooling-pads that you can put in the freezer, and you can put aloe vera on them and they sound amazing.

First Sex:
You aren't supposed to have sex for the first six weeks after giving birth for a lot of reasons, the major reason being your body just went through a major shift and needs to heal before putting anything else in it, even if it's supposed to be pleasurable. My first time back was uncomfortable, but it was nice to have that connection back with my husband. At this time, I wasn't aware of how important it is to heal and re-strengthen your pelvic floor. The pelvic floor is a funnel-shaped structure that attaches to the walls of the lesser pelvis, separating the pelvic cavity from the genitalia and anus. Three years later I was still having pain during sex that the doctor couldn't explain other than things shifting around. I began to do pelvic floor breathing and exercises and the pain magically went away. I had no pain in my cervix or my vagina during sex anymore.

One thing I cannot go without saying is you should have a plan for your next baby. If you are not ready to have another baby, get on birth control as soon as you can and wait to have sex until you are on it. You can start ovulating as soon as three weeks after giving birth and just pause for a second, can you imagine having two babies in one year?

It's possible and it's called having Irish twins. I chose to get on birth control as soon as I could, and my husband also got a vasectomy after our second. Some people are even told that if you breast feed, it's considered 100% birth control. Well just keep in mind, that's not always true. We knew we were done and literally could not imagine being able to survive having a third.

First Time Sitting Down:

This is one of the few things I remember in agonizing detail. Although something as simple as walking or sitting after giving birth seems so insignificant, it is a major unexpected adjustment. It feels very similar to going on a long bike ride in an uncomfortable seat. I thought we had a soft couch, but when I sat down for the first time it felt like I was sitting on a bunch of pointy rocks, and I struggled to get comfortable. Walking felt very similar to post running a marathon; your legs are shaky and your whole-body hurts. I felt like Ariel The Little Mermaid walking out of the water for the first time to the real-world, tripping over myself in pain.

First time looking in the mirror:

After labor I immediately put a bellyband around my stomach to hold everything together and speed up the healing process. I wrapped it so tight around my stomach and I also wrapped another one around my hips because if you didn't have hips before having a baby, let me tell you, you do now! It's a weird feeling in your stomach right after you give birth and walk around. Your stomach feels like it's going to fall out of your vagina. The belly band really helps with this and helps your body recover faster. Physically I felt good when I had it on but mentally, I felt like a whale.

Whose job is it to tell you that you should throw away every preconceived notion you had about getting your pre-pregnancy body back, once the baby is out? "I thought I was fit before the pregnancy so my body will know what to do," "I'll work out as soon as I can and get fit again," "I'll eat healthy, rest, exercise, do all the things," but when you look in the mirror, the psychological concept that your body will snap back is outweighed by the fact that the actual postpartum body is no joke.

You look in the mirror and for a long time, I mean months, you still look pregnant! Psychologically seeing yourself pregnant for nine months isn't fun, and then after getting the baby out you still have 15-20 pounds of pooch hanging down from your stomach. When you first work out, your body acts as if you are a baby calf learning to walk. It's not easy either physically or emotionally and I think this was one of the contributing factors to my postpartum depression.

When I had kids, celebrities were shown snapping back immediately after. Just recently in 2023, some celebrities have shown what reality is, like Chrissy Teigen posting pictures of her immediately after giving birth showing what reality looks like. Bless her soul for being honest and helping spread the word that it is a necessity to take time to recover and it is normal to not fit a preconceived definition of "normal."

First Time Going Outside:

Going outside was a huge deal for my mental health. You wouldn't think it would be, but being cooped up in the house with the baby every second of the day weighs on you in ways you don't realize until it's too late. My husband and I would take the baby on a daily walk, even if it was just once around the park, down the street, or even just up and down our driveway, either carrying him or taking him in the stroller. I remember feeling so free that I could breathe for just a second. I didn't have to feed, change, rock the baby, I could just go outside and enjoy the cool air on my face or the sun beating down on me.

I'll go into this later, but while I didn't feel a major connection to the baby, I had constant anxiety that something bad was going to happen to him. I worried that he would stop breathing, that someone would break in and take him, that he'd get too cold, or roll over and not be able to breathe, that someone would drop him, that I wouldn't hear him in the middle of the night, or he would have some sort of defect.

I had huge feelings of doubt and dread about myself, like I couldn't be a mother, especially not for the rest of my life. It was too much pressure; it was too much for me to handle and I didn't want anything to do with it. My family would tease me and say, "I'll just take him home and take care of him," and I would honestly answer and say "Okay, do it."

Of course, they would laugh jokingly, and I would give my husband an apologetic look, because we both knew I meant it. I wanted little to do with him if I wasn't feeding him. I didn't want to hold him, rock him, or sing to him. I just couldn't.

I would find myself crying for no reason while I was sitting in my rocking chair feeding the baby. My husband would come in and check if I needed anything and I would be crying so hard I could barely breathe. He would ask if I was okay and I would say, yes, and there wasn't anything he could do for me because not only did I not know why I was crying, I couldn't really stop it until my body was done letting it all out. It was at this time that I didn't realize I was in what they call the 4th trimester.

"When God created mothers, He made her to stretch.
Not just her physical body, but her emotional capacity.
She feels it all.
He stretched her heart so it had room for each child He blessed her with.
He stretched her mind as she carries all of the mental load and the worries.
And he stretched her ability to love because a mother's love is one of a kind.
She wasn't made to bend or break – she was made to stretch."
~Courtney Devich

CHAPTER 11

What Even is Real Life

What Is Dissociation?

Dissociation refers to being disconnected from the present moment. It is a subconscious way of coping with and avoiding a traumatic situation or negative thoughts. When a person experiences dissociation, they become disconnected from their surroundings or from themselves. This reaction works to temporarily alleviate potentially overwhelming emotional experiences such as traumatic memories and may temporarily reduce feelings of shame, anxiety, or fear—but it doesn't function as a healthy long-term fix.

The first couple of days after labor were a blur that nobody prepared me for. So, I'm going to try and prepare you! It was around eight months after the baby was born that I told my husband I was going to try to go to therapy, because something wasn't right. I wish someone would've recognized the signs and symptoms earlier to push me to go to get help.

Some of the symptoms that I had were feeling sad, hopeless, and overwhelmed. For me, this was crying at random times, crying during breast-feeding, crying if the dishes weren't done, crying because my husband had to work, lots of crying. Most of the time this was in private because I was trying not to let people know I was crying.

The enemy wants you to feel like nobody else is going through what you are, that you are all alone in your journey, and nobody is on your side. Boy did I feel this during this time period. I know it's irrational now, like really? Nobody else has gone through this other than me? I realized God is not against me. I expected him to show up in a certain way and even though he may not be showing up the way you expected him to, doesn't mean he's not there at all.

He's in it with you, working through you, and fighting for you every step of the way. You just need to open your soul and accept the holy spirit. It doesn't have to be a huge miracle that God creates. It can be in the small things. Like if a friend you haven't spoken to in a while reaches out. If you were able to get up and go on a walk that day. If you see a rainbow, a shooting star, a penny or feather from heaven, family helping out, your baby actually sleeping, your able to take a shower! Finding joy in the little things is extremely important and remembering God is always on your side no matter what.

So, if you see a parent who has red puffy eyes, really check in with them and ask how they are doing. If they say fine or good, don't believe them and ask more prodding questions. For example, ask if they are sad, ask if they are overwhelmed with anything, ask if they've been crying a lot, ask if they want help or just want you to listen.

Another symptom I had was obsessive thoughts about the baby. Some people have obsessive thoughts of hurting themselves or the baby but for me, it was obsessive thoughts that something bad was going to happen to the baby like someone was going to walk up and steal them at the grocery store or park, my family members were going to accidently drop them, I was going to leave them in the car, they would choke on their milk, they would go to sleep and not wake up, just a lot of unrealistic thoughts that something bad was going to happen. My family probably thought I was a little too overprotective or being silly, but this is another sign that something isn't normal.

One of my most important feelings that I wish people would've noticed is me not having interest in the baby. It was small things that I did and didn't notice until looking back that I would call the baby "it" instead of him or her and I wouldn't want to hold them.

When I breastfed, I wasn't interested. I didn't have eye contact, stroke their little baby nose, sing to them, or cuddle them. I literally just plopped them on, fed them, and gave them away. It never felt real to me that the baby was mine. I felt like I was raising my husband's baby.

I also had zero energy or motivation for anything because I was so exhausted from everything. This turned into me forgetting to eat, unintentionally skipping meals or just taking a few bites and going to do something else. My husband would have to remind me constantly to drink water, eat food, basic things I should've been prioritizing.

There's this test called the Edinburgh Postnatal Depression Scale that asks you a series of ten questions on how the person feels during the last seven days. This test will tell you if you are most likely suffering from depression or post-partum based on your answers to the test. I remember taking this test at my doctor's office during a follow up however I think because I didn't even realize I was having the symptoms; it would've been helpful to fill it out together with my husband so I could answer a little closer to how I was feeling but also how others were seeing me. I think this is a great tool to utilize to start a conversation. You can easily find this test online and if you have questions about it or the symptoms it references, this is your chance to ask your doctor and start that conversation.

I don't remember how I got connected with my therapist, but when I first went to her office, it was familiar and comfortable because it wasn't the first time I'd been to therapy. There is nothing like being alone with a third party, telling them all of your thoughts and feelings and hoping not to be judged. I immediately told her what was going on and how, from the very start of getting pregnant, it didn't seem real. I told her how it was transferring to other things, how the baby didn't feel like mine, our house didn't feel like mine and my life didn't feel like mine.

Dissociation Anxiety Disorder.

That is what my therapist diagnosed me as having. When the therapist explained it to me, I finally felt like someone got me. Someone understood everything that I was going through and was putting words to it. I wasn't alone and I wasn't crazy. I was very fortunate to have worked very hard with my therapist to realize this.

You should see the faces you get when people think you are living the "perfect" life. You have a nice car, house, husband, career, kids, the list goes on and on. You should feel happy and appreciative, but I didn't feel anything at all. I just felt lost, like I was living someone else's life, and I didn't have any choice. I was just going through the motions to keep up appearances.

You know it's weird, but right after the baby arrives you are cut off from everything you are used to, and everything you know. One day you are kissing your husband goodbye as you go off to work, and the next, you don't have work, you don't talk to your friends, you can't go out, and it's hard to even look in the mirror.

I know I talked a little bit earlier about physical changes but there is nothing that can prepare you for the changes you will see in the mirror after giving birth. Someone once told me, "You'll never get your pre-baby body back," and I'm still trying to prove them wrong to this day. My hips expanded once I got pregnant to adjust to hold the extra weight. My boobs got bigger from breast-feeding, which is nice of course at first, but after breast-feeding is done, they look like deflated punching bags and even though I don't have big boobs, it's still a hit to the ego. I had stretchmarks everywhere, but mostly on my belly and thighs. My rib cage expanded so I had to wear bra extenders. My hair was falling out. I had dark circles under my eyes from not sleeping at night. My stomach was a big round ball of mush, ready to fall out with any sudden movement if it wasn't wrapped up in a corset so tight, I couldn't breathe.

With all these changes to your body, it's no wonder it's hard to feel like yourself after childbirth. One look in the mirror and I had no idea who was staring back at me.

I always wanted to be a mother but not like this. Not like this little girl staring back, screaming for help on the inside, behind a big bright smile. I kept thinking over and over, why didn't we wait, why did we want kids in the first place, was this all even worth it? I cannot take care of this little human for the rest of my life.

My life is over!

This feeling really reminds me of the song from the Disney movie *Encanto* where the sister Luisa holds everything on her back, both metaphorically and literally.

"What breaks the camel's back?
It's pressure like a drip, drip, drip, that'll never stop, whoa.
Pressure that'll tip, tip tip, 'til you just go pop!
See if she can hang on a little longer,
Who am I if I can't carry it all? If I falter?
Under the surface, I hide my nerves and it worsens,
I worry something is gonna hurt us, under the surface.
I think about my purpose, can I somehow preserve this?
Line up the dominoes, a light wind blows, you try to stop it tumbling but
on and on it goes.
But wait, if I could shake the crushing weight of expectations,
Would that free some room up for joy? Or Relaxation? Or simple
pleasure?
Instead we measure this growing pressure.
Keep growing, keep going.

No cracks, no breaks, no mistakes, no pressure."

The pressure of other's expectations when you become pregnant—of who you should be as a mother, daughter, friend, worker or how you should feel, or what you should be doing—is exhausting, literally exhausting.

What really gets me is that there is nowhere easy to turn for help. The doctor has you fill out these forms each time you come in for a checkup after labor, but it's clear they're screening for postpartum depression. They are obvious questions like, have you thought about harming yourself? Have you cried for more than ten minutes for no reason? Have you thought about harming the baby? Most of these answers were no for me, as I didn't have it that bad, but you feel almost pointed out and shamed for feeling that way even if it's the doctor asking.

When I filled out the forms, I told the doctor that I wasn't having a lot of those symptoms, but I didn't feel like me and something was wrong. She told me that I was brave to even bring it up, and that it was most likely either baby blues or postpartum depression. I had no idea what either of those were, even though I had heard about them before. But nobody ever told me to expect this. I think society is progressing quicker to be able to inform mothers and parents about this but in the past, people who had just had a baby would just literally go crazy and then be put into a psych ward without ever getting correctly diagnosed.

For your reference the biggest difference is the baby blues come and go, but postpartum last longer and have a much bigger impact on your ability to function, mentally and physically.

Between giving birth and four weeks, 80%--let me say that again, 80%--of new moms have the baby blues and up to 20% of moms develop postpartum mood disorders.

Women who have had a pregnancy and

postpartum mental health illness are 50% more likely to have it with their next pregnancy.

800,000 women will suffer from a pregnancy or postpartum mental health illness in the United States each year.

Only 15% of women with pregnancy and postpartum mental health illness are diagnosed.

Over 20% of postpartum deaths are caused by suicide.

African American women suffer at rates 35% percent higher than the rest of the population.

1 in 10 dads will experience a perinatal mental health disorder after the birth of their child.

And zero percent of people in my world talked or warned me about any of this.

Most of the time after a few weeks, hormone levels adjust and the blues disappear, but for some it's not that easy. So, piling on top of physical changes, mental changes, and "all the things," you now have to worry about hormonal changes that can affect you like postpartum depression. I read that once you have a baby your brain literally changes. The grey matter in your brain shrinks! The changes can last up to two years after childbirth. This can affect things like your vision, hearing, emotions, and decision making. This part softens so that other parts of your brain make sure you can attend to your baby's needs. This can potentially cause hypervigilance which wears you down even more.

I started counting the days until I could go back to work and not be around or watch the baby. I'd dread the time until I had to pump or feed again. I'd cringe every time the baby would fuss because I knew it was time to feed. I was terrified every time we left the house because that meant all the pressure was on me to provide food for the baby, and who knew if my body would cooperate, or if I would feel weird stripping down and breast-feed right then and there.

I was scared I'd have vertigo again. I was frightened thinking about being the sole provider for our child. I felt unsafe to be left alone with the baby when my husband went back to work and had all those same fears crop up again. Little did I know this was a sign of obsessive-compulsive perinatal disorder.

How can I do this by myself? How can someone trust me with the kids without any training or knowledge? I felt embarrassed to go back to work because it felt like everyone could see through to the real me who was slowly fading away.

When I ended up going back to work, I had to figure out childcare. Sometimes my parents would watch the baby and other times I was lucky enough to stay home during the days my husband had to work. Even though I was ready to go back to work, the separation anxiety was real. I felt guilty for leaving the baby with someone else and at the same time I felt guilty for wanting to go to back to work and be away from the baby. It was a no-win situation.

I had to force myself to stay present in the moment. When I was at work, I focused on work and getting things done. When I was at home, I focused on spending time with the baby. It's true what Michelle. Obama says, "You can have it all but not at the same time. No one has it all and why should we?" You are always making a choice and missing out on something. If you are rocking it at work, you are missing your baby's first steps. When you are an awesome mom at home, you are missing out on that important meeting that you should've been leading or a promotion. Either way you will be making a choice and it's up to you to decide what is important to you and what you can mentally and physically handle.

Once you set your boundaries, stick with them and be confident in your choice. Your work will benefit when you are completely focused on work instead of your kids. Your kids will benefit from you being present when you are with them and focused on the present instead of worrying about the past or the future.

Michelle Obama also said, "Being a mother made me a better professional, because coming home every night to my girls reminded me what I was working for. And being a professional made me a better mother, because pursuing my dreams, I was modeling for my girls how to pursue their dreams."

It's harder than it sounds but meditation and intention will help. Even if it's turning off your phone, setting it down for ten minutes, and fully being present. Letting go of all external unrealistic expectations. If you want to work from home and your employer lets you, work from home! If you want to go into the office and your children go to daycare all day, do it! Show yourself some grace as you figure out the best path for you and a little at a time will help.

There is a scene in the show *Working Mom's* where the mom comes face to face with a bear in the woods while she's running with her child. She stops stunned, pauses, and slowly steps in front of the stroller while putting herself between the bear and her kids. Then she does the unthinkable and the opposite of what most would do and screams at the top of her lungs. It was such an impactful and unexpected scene.

The creator Catherine Reitman says, "The bear was just this incredible manifestation of all the fears we have to overcome, not just as working mothers, but as women. There are these monsters that appear and stop you in your tracks and want to take away everything you have worked for."

You will have a chance to stare the "bear" right in the face and be able to let it all out, in hopes you are doing the right thing for your child. This may look like crying in your car uncontrollably when you leave to go back to work for the first day. It may manifest as separation anxiety stopping you from leaving the house, or maybe even leaving the city if you are traveling. It may feel like joy when dropping them off to daycare for the first time. It may be wanting to be with your child all the time because you can't handle the cuteness. It may feel like relief when you go back to work or it may feel like a deep yearning to be with your baby all the time. There is no such thing as "normal."

No matter the feelings, know that you are not crazy, and you are not a bad mom. You are just you. And you are not your feelings.

On top of all these "feelings", I didn't feel like myself. I felt like I had become who everyone else wanted me to be. I had all these "perfect" things on the outside, but on the inside, I didn't know who I was. I didn't feel like a mom. I didn't feel like I should even *be* a mom. I didn't feel like a wife. I didn't feel like any choice in my life was mine.

"So do not fear
For I am
WITH YOU
Do not be dismayed
For I am
YOUR GOD
I will strengthen
You and help you."

Isaiah 41:10

CHAPTER 12

Light at the End of the Tunnel

For a long time, I felt like society's compliant daughter. The daughter who says yes, ma'am, and yes, sir. The daughter who has a child and a happy loving family and shouldn't complain about anything. 

What I truly felt, or what I wanted, didn't matter any longer. As long as I was portraying a happy persona on the outside, everyone was happy to go about their business like everything was okay. This happened more so with my first baby than my second.

I remember my husband telling me, "Please don't forget the baby in the car," or asking me if I felt like leaving the baby in the shopping cart and walking away. I had to reassure him, but I could tell, deep down, he was really worried about me and wanted me to get the help I needed.

Through working most of this out with my therapist weekly, we concluded together that most of my feelings of dread were coming from the fact that I was the sole provider of nourishment for the baby. I felt like nobody else in the world could give the baby what he needed except me, which made me feel like someone who had been kidnapped and put in handcuffs for the rest of my life. I literally felt at the time like it would never end, and I'd never be myself again, never be able to leave the house feeling normal again, never see my friends again, never go to work or feel like someone contributing to society.

My therapist asked me what I had been doing to feed the baby, and why. I told her I had been breast-feeding because I knew it was better for the baby. Even though I felt like a cow whose sole purpose was just to get her baby milk and that's it. She asked me how long I wanted to do that, and I told her a year, and she asked why, again, and I couldn't give her an answer. I told her, if I didn't breastfeed, my family would look down on me, or people would look down on me because I was weak and couldn't last that long.

In working this out with my therapist, we decided it would be best for me to try to wean the baby off breast-feeding and exclusively pump. That my feelings of potential disappointment from family and others was an unfair expectation before even allowing them to respond.

All I could think, was that someone gave me an out, and if I didn't take it right at that moment, I would lose my chance. I came home and explained to my husband what was going on, and he completely supported me. We researched the best formula we could find, and I think I slowly weaned to just bottle feeding in under a week.

When this happened, I felt free. I felt like the *Sound of Music* girl twirling on top of the hill. I no longer dreaded the baby crying because I had started to build up a stash of milk. My husband was able to get up in the middle of the night to help with feedings. I was able to get some sleep and was no longer exhausted. I could pump at work and not feel guilty about not feeding the baby.

And once I knew the baby was fine, I let go of all that guilt.

Ten months is what I lasted for the first baby through breast-feeding at home and pumping at work. Two months of formula to make it to a year.

Pumping at work was a lot more awkward than I thought it would be. I had to ask my boss at the time if I could take a couple of breaks during the day to pump. I would have to put 20-minute meetings on my calendar as a reminder to go pump because I would be so involved with work I would forget and get engorged. I would put a little sticky on my door so people would know where I was because I was so afraid people were going to judge me for not working the entire time and being missing if my butt wasn't in the chair.

I was fortunate that we did have a special room for pumping, but you'd have to be lucky to sign up and get the time slot you needed. I just used an old office close to my cubicle that had a locked door and booked that room for the time. Of course, this was also awkward because people didn't always know what I was doing in there, especially my male coworkers. I made do and used it as a true break from work to catch up on life, breathe a little, and know that what I was doing was a super-power no matter what people may be thinking.

But my second child got a full year of breast milk through my pumping exclusively after the first week.

One is not better than the other in my opinion. Each experience is different for each individual and the best decision is a well-fed baby. Period. I have bonded with both regardless.

Doctors should not be pushing so hard for breast-feeding, but rather a physically and mentally healthy baby *and* mama no matter what the avenue you decide on as a parent.

"Grief is not a sign of
WEAKNESS

nor a lack of

Faith —

It is the price of
LOVE"
~Unknown

CHAPTER 13

Sometimes the Smallest Things Take up the Most Room in Your Heart

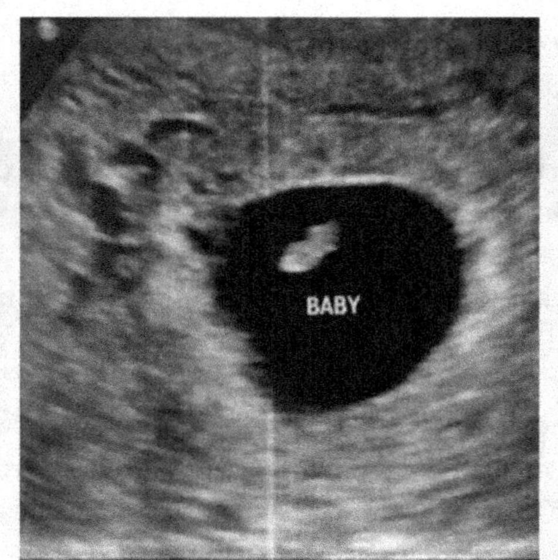

OUR BABY ANGEL MARIANO AT 6 WEEKS.
I'M SO GRATEFUL TO HAVE CAPTURED AT
LEAST ONE IMAGE BEFORE WE HAD OUR
MISCARRIAGE.

We, as mothers, are always running. Running to the next activity for your child, the next play date, date night, friend's night, meeting, celebration, doctor's appointment, sporting event, and on and on and on. Not until after I had my first child, did I realize I took my ability to run, for granted. When I became pregnant for the second time, I couldn't keep running like I was used to. I knew that once I had my baby, it would be so much harder to start running again after having two kids.

Running has always been my way of releasing stress and tension so that I didn't feel like I was suffocating in my own skin.

Then as quickly as the pregnancy had come, between my two kids, I had a miscarriage, 12 weeks in. It hit me like a speeding bullet.

Unexpected and deadly.

I remember being in the doctor's office for just another routine checkup. Thank goodness my husband was with me, because when it was time to hear the heartbeat, the doctor squeezed that little cream on my belly and rubbed the little machine to find the heartbeat and:

Silence.

Pure terrifying silence.

My heart started racing and I could see the doctor becoming a little more anxious and impatient because there was no sound coming from the machine. I reached out for my husband's hand and tried not to start crying, because there was nothing wrong in my mind.

Then the doctor told me, "For some reason I can't find the heartbeat so let's get the other machine and try, sometimes the babies like to hide, and we just can't find it. No need to worry… yet."

She tried again with the next machine, and I knew once I saw it. The little bean of a baby was sitting at the bottom of my uterus, motionless. I remembered my first baby was like a little Mexican jumping bean, freely and joyfully jumping around with the tiniest of movements. This one was not moving. I couldn't breathe. The doctor was sweating. My husband's hand was squeezing mine.

Then we heard it. The loudest, most obnoxious, silence.

The doctor said, "I cannot find the heartbeat and it looks like you've lost the baby. I'm so, so sorry."

I almost wanted to say, "Well then, go and find it if it's lost!" But I didn't.

Instead, I sat there having this weird realization that there was something inside of me that was no longer alive.

I was telling myself to breathe repeatedly, that it was going to be ok. I had so many different emotions running through me and I was scared because I had no idea what that meant for me and my body.

Not to mention I panicked to tell our family because they were all so excited to have another baby in the family. I remember telling my grandma over the phone and just hearing her scream, "NOOOOO!" My heart sank for her.

I was scared that my husband would be mad at me, like it was my fault somehow. I was frustrated to have to go through the whole pregnancy thing again if we wanted to have another baby. I was thankful that we never mentioned anything to my little boy so he wouldn't be confused. I was shocked because I didn't truly consider this as a possibility. I was frustrated that, not once, did anyone warn me or tell me what the statistics of having a miscarriage were. At the time, I was mad that God let this happen to us.

Having a miscarriage is a spontaneous loss of pregnancy, often because the fetus isn't developing normally. You can have blood, fluid, or tissue coming from the vagina and pain in the belly. 10-15% of pregnancies end in miscarriage and most happen in the 1st trimester before the twelfth week. If you are older, there is a greater chance of having a pregnancy loss.

I've never liked the title "miscarriage." It implies that your body didn't do something right and the carrying of the baby didn't work. This is not the case, and you didn't do anything wrong. It's your body doing what it needs to do to survive.

After talking with my husband and asking him how he felt, he very calmly told me that it was meant to be and there was nothing we could do about it. He has never been one to show much emotion. But when I started thinking like that, it really helped. I don't control the universe; God does, and who am I to think that He was wrong in allowing this to happen.

I knew it was part of a greater plan, even though it was not our plan.

But the unexpectedness of the news, combined with the excitement that I would be able to run again, left me paralyzed. I didn't know how I was supposed to feel. I didn't realize that, even though you may have had a miscarriage, your body still thinks you are pregnant for a while after. Which could be dangerous if it goes on too long.

I was lucky enough that we were only around 12 weeks along and I wouldn't have needed a surgical procedure called Dilation and Curettage (D&C). D&C is a procedure to remove tissue from inside your uterus.

Even though that was a relief, I still had to take *Misoprostol* pills to make the miscarriage happen and ensure my uterus was empty. I had to go for multiple blood tests after to see if my hormone levels had dropped to the expected rate. I had to follow up with my doctor. I had to do another ultrasound to make sure everything was clear. Going through this process was very strange. I felt like, every time I went to pee, the baby was coming out of me from all the excess fluids coming out from my uterus and I had such a weird, guilty feeling. But I kept telling myself, this is the way it's supposed to be, it's just my body clearing out and making sure I'm okay. After having a miscarriage there is no perfect time to wait to conceive again but the doctors encouraged us to wait a few months to make sure your body is strong enough to have another potential healthy pregnancy.

Mark Manson says, "The desire for a more positive experience, is itself, a negative experience and paradoxically, the acceptance of one's negative experience is, itself, a positive experience."

I heard this quote two years after my last child, and it finally clicked for me. I had always wanted a different experience with pregnancy, labor, and breast-feeding. I wanted everything about the whole "having a baby" experience to be and feel different than it had been. But when I heard this quote I realized, God put me here to have this one unique experience. It may not have been what I wanted or expected, but I was right where God wanted me, for whatever reason. He knew what he was doing, and I came out a better person for my own experience.

My son has always had a close relationship with God and is often aware of things we are not. We never told our son that we were pregnant, so after we had our miscarriage, he kept pointing upward around our house telling us he saw a baby angel and getting frustrated that we couldn't see the angel. It would happen at totally random times, in the bathtub, at dinner, watching TV.

One day, we were all sitting on the couch, and he did it again so we asked, "What's their name?" and my son said "Anano."

My husband asked "Mariano?" and my son excitedly said, "YES!"

We never knew the gender of our baby so we had chosen a name that could be either gender. We chose Mariano or Mariana.

My son was waving and talking to our baby.

Angels are real and they are all around us. This gave me a little sense of peace to know that our baby was okay and even though they were gone they were not lost.

"Most of us have enough areas in our lives where we have to meet others' expectations. Let your running be about your own
HOPES
&
DREAMS."
~Meb Keflezighi~

CHAPTER 14

In it For the Long Run

AFTER FINISHING MY MARATHON. I WAS
EXHAUSTED BUT I KNEW MY SON WOULD
LOOK UP TO ME ONE DAY AND BE PROUD
FOR WHAT I ACCOMPLISHED.

That summer after my miscarriage, I had a few trips planned. The first was really hard.

One of my good friends was having a bachelorette party that weekend right after we found out we had a miscarriage. Of course, I wanted to go but didn't realize the impact a miscarriage has on your body and how it would affect me. I had to wear a pad because of the random bleeding. And to top it all off, we were going to a hot-spring, which I couldn't get in the hot springs because of the possibility of bacterial infection.

I had to tell her what was going on, because I didn't want to feel like the odd man out, being the only one not to get into the hot springs. Again, I felt so much guilt wanting to go on this trip to celebrate my friend, all the while leaving my baby at home.

I'm not sure at what point in time we begin feeling guilty about being away from our kids, or about not being there every second of the day. I think part of it is societal pressure that if we are posting on social media about living life outside of our kids, we get labeled as a bad mom or bad parents. People saying, "I can't believe she is over there partying or going out while she leaves the baby at home."

I think it's extremely important to remember we are a person - then we are a mother.

We had our own unique identity before becoming a mother. We had friends before becoming a mother. We had hopes and dreams before becoming a mother. We had a life outside of being a mother.

And we need to put on our oxygen mask first to take time to focus on ourselves before we can be the best mom to our kids.

So, this trip was me dipping my toe into the conscientious decision of taking care of myself, first. I needed time away from everyone to truly heal from the pain of having a miscarriage. I needed to rest and have fun while celebrating my friend.

I had another bachelorette trip celebrating my friend where I needed time with my friends to have deep long talks about life, love, and reminisce about the past and dream about the future. I needed to be me without any external forces telling me who I should be, what decisions I should be making, or what I should be doing.

Another trip that Summer was to Washington D.C. for a business trip. All in all, everything went fine, until we got to the airport to come back home, and our flight was canceled. It was just chance that I was the last of my coworkers to the counter when they told me there were no other seats on the flight until later that night. I was so heartbroken because this was one of the first times, I had left my son behind.

Again, I felt guilty that I wasn't able to come home. I felt guilty for leaving him with my husband longer than intended. Part of me did feel like this little six-hour window of time before my next plane was leaving was a chance to explore who I was in a different city without answering to anyone. But I even felt guilty about looking at it that way. At least, at first.

After booking what seemed like the latest flight in the world and the last one out of the city, I made a decision. Before having kids, I would've sat in the airport and watched something online to pass the time. I would've felt sorry for myself and complained the entire time to my husband. But instead of wasting my time, I chose to live my life to the fullest. I jumped right into the cab and called my husband to tell him what happened, bawling my eyes out for the guilt. I got it all out.

I rode the cab back to our hotel, changed my clothes, and left my suitcase with the concierge. I paused for a second to think through what I wanted to do with the next six hours, and I decided to explore museums, libraries, and eat the biggest burger I could find.

I went through the museum by myself taking pictures with a volunteer from the museum because she felt bad for me. Ha! I had such a good time navigating D.C. by myself that it was sort of a metaphor in my mind of being able to navigate motherhood on my own, without anyone giving me advice or telling me what I should be doing or how I should be doing it.

Even though it was tough, I got through these trips and started to slowly find myself again.

I believe it was the silence during this time of spending quality time with myself and God that made this change so crucial for me. I realized that the time I took to reflect and have a positive attitude makes a difference. I realized being present in each moment is how life is intended. I realized God listened to me and had my back more than I knew or was aware of.

During these trips that Summer, I realized I could begin making decisions for myself that could impact my trajectory in life. I could do what I wanted, even though I had kids. I could do what I was yearning for, to please myself, and myself alone. I didn't have to live up to anyone else's expectations of being the "good girl," the "good wife," the "good mother." Those who were my true friends understood me and held me with open arms. They let me cry, love, laugh, and be me.

For the first time in my life, I felt in control of myself. I wasn't letting other people determine who I was or should be. This feeling—one I had never felt before—

was similar to the feeling I had when I free fell from the Stratosphere in Las Vegas, Nevada when I was twenty-one and again at thirty-one. It's like the world around you is out of control but you feel so present and confident in your own body. I know Alicia Keys talks about this as your "knowing." You feel your place in the world. You feel like something inside of you clicks and everything just makes sense.

It was like everything in the world was surrounding me but somehow, I was also surrounding it.

It was as if the Holy Spirit was circling around and holding me, guiding me to the right path in my life. A few people guided me to get there and helped push me along the way.

I could just be me.

Unequivocal and unapologetically, me.

Since I was able to run again after healing from having kids, I was really trying to find out who I was, not as a mom, daughter, wife, sister, or friend; but as Mariah, Rye, Mur, or any other name that I've gone by. Little did I know that I would accomplish the biggest achievement in my life later that year.

Once I overcame the loss of the baby, I had a deep yearning for something more in my life.

I started to search for running races I could complete. I had already completed a half marathon, so I pushed myself to do a longer run. I was astonished to see how many races were available to run! The list was literally endless. The one that caught my eye was the 'Sandia Crest Marathon'.

Without hesitation, I signed up and within minutes, I started training. At first, I'd just run around the block. Then I would run down some of the main roads in Albuquerque, until eventually I was driving to the highest point in the city at the base of the Sandia Mountains and running all the way home. Thirteen miles later, I'd arrive home, my body falling apart, but my mind on fire.

Running through the different neighborhoods and seeing the diverse landscapes, houses, and people, made me so joyful. It helped me realize the world was so much bigger than my neighborhood that I grew up in.

I played soccer most of my life and absolutely loved it. I never used to like the running aspect of it, or at least I didn't appreciate it until after it was gone. Now, training almost ten years later, I felt free when I ran. I didn't have to compete with anyone other than my mind. When my body was done, my mind took over and gave me the strength to complete whatever training run I needed to do that day.

I think prepping for a marathon is much harder than completing the actual marathon. Race day came around and I felt prepared; prepared for this major event that I felt would define the rest of my life. This was not just another run or marathon for me. It was bigger than that. It was proving to myself that I could do anything I wanted, and that I was more. I was more than how people choose to define me, more than just a mom, a wife, a daughter, a sister, a coworker, etc.

Although I trained mostly alone, I was far from alone on race day. The bus pulled up to the starting line at the top of the Sandia Crest and it was nothing like I had ever imagined. Music was blaring, runners were wearing heat blankets dancing in the dark, there was an emcee hyping up the crowd, and there seemed to be an endless drop-off of runners each time the bus returned. I was surrounded by runners from, not only Albuquerque, but all over the United States. I had never felt such comradery from people with a common goal. We were all chasing the runner's high where just as you think you can't go any further, your body transforms into something you don't recognize, your lungs become powerful, your legs feel light, and you feel like you could endlessly fly down the mountain.

This was the hardest, most challenging thing my mind and my body has ever been through. If it wasn't for the beautiful sunrise before the race started, the long windy downhill roads lined with the tallest trees, the view overlooking the city, the cars honking in support as we passed main roads, and all the other runners surrounding me, I'm not sure I would've made it.

Six hours later, I got a text from my husband telling me to hurry up if I wanted to make it to the finish line in time, so I threw my butt in second gear. Every bone and muscle in my body hurt and my mind kept playing tricks on me, but I knew my family would be there cheering me on when I got to the finish line.

My two great friends were there cheering me on and surprised me with the best and biggest signs a girl could ask for. One sign said, "I bet you thought this was a good idea six months ago!" and another said, "Go Mariah!" My boss even showed up and surprised me halfway through and gave me a little pep talk to get me through to the end!

There are times like these where the people who care about you the most are the people who show up. It doesn't matter if they have kids, if they're single, if you've been friends your whole life, or if you just met them.

The people who truly care about you as a person will always show up.

I will always remember how proud my two-year-old was when he saw me come through the finish line. He stood there wearing a shirt my husband surprised me by making him that said, "RUN MOM RUN!" He held my hand as proud as he could be, letting everyone take pictures of us together.

At this point in time, Allyson Felix said it best when explaining how she made a comeback in the Olympics after having her daughter. She said, "I was running for so much more than for medals or a time on the track. I was running for a representation of women, for mothers, and for anybody who has been told their story was over."

So, when you see me crossing that finish line, know that I'm not perfect, I'm not always happy, I don't "have it all." This marathon is only the beginning of my journey. I cannot wait to celebrate this pivotal moment in my life surrounded by people I love.

Through all the anxiety, training, pain, injuries, massages, and workouts, I know it will all be worth it.

"*SOMETIMES BEING A BROTHER IS EVEN BETTER THAN BEING A SUPERHERO.*"
~UNKNOWN

CHAPTER 15

Second Time's the Charm

At this time in my life, I was finally coming to terms with being called "mommy" and knew how to keep myself grounded. I had conquered our schedule with a new baby, I had dealt with the separation anxiety, the postpartum depression, the inadequacies of trying to be a mother, a wife, a working mom, a friend, a daughter.

But just when I thought we were in a good place, we found out we were pregnant a third time. At first, I had all the same feelings of joy and pure intimidation. I knew I didn't want to allow myself to be too happy or hopeful because having our miscarriage felt like the rug had been pulled out from under us.

I certainly did not want that to happen again.

Every time we went in for a check up to the doctor, I'd almost have an anxiety attack because the fear of losing another baby was overwhelmingly sickening. Each time we went in, it got worse and worse. I have never prayed more in my life than during that pregnancy. I know it might sound horrible to some, but I was praying for both the baby to be healthy as I wanted to raise another child of God, but I was also praying for the baby to be healthy so that I wouldn't have to go through pregnancy, labor, and postpartum again.

Thankfully, this pregnancy and delivery was a lot easier the second time around because I had already gone through everything once, I knew what to expect. We knew where to go at the hospital, we knew how the labor room looked, we knew when to go to the hospital, we knew what my physical and emotional psyche would most likely be, we knew what to expect after the delivery. I've heard a lot that you can't really understand what it feels like until you've actually been through it, and boy is that true. I could

explain every little detail to you about my experience, but it still wouldn't be enough to prepare you, because our story is our story and yours will be unique to you.
But this time around, we felt prepared, we felt like we were a team, we felt we could do anything!

I remember as we were waiting in the hospital while I was in labor, we began to see news stories on how a disease was starting to spread in China. But we didn't think anything of it. One, because it was China, and two, because I was in pain!

We brought my daughter home from the hospital, knowing it was going to be important how we introduced her to our son, who was three years old at the time. We would tell him that he was responsible for loving her and showing her how to be a baby. He had the most important job. My mom was watching him when we brought my daughter home. He was the cutest with her. He wasn't quite sure about it, but he wanted to hold her and love her from the very beginning. I remember him just looking at her in awe like she was his, forever. He would stroke her little hands and face and just say how cute she was.
From that moment on he had met his true love.

If you remember, we'd told our family we needed a week to get situated with our new family and to make sure we were all comfortable with this change before we had a ton of visitors like the first time. This is probably one of the best things I could recommend to anybody who is having more than one child. Make sure your kids feel safe and comfortable before giving everyone else what they want.

Naturally, I tried to research as much as I could before having two kids so that I could be successful in how happy we were as a family. Naturally as a Type-A personality would.

I got each of them a gift from each other so that they knew they were cared about. I was very careful with my words so that my son didn't feel like he came second or was being ignored "for the baby." We tried not to say things like, "I can't right now I'm with the baby," or "the baby needs to eat first." We were very specific with our language. For example, if my son asked us to play, we would say, "I would love to play with you. As soon as I'm done feeding the baby, we can do whatever you want." This seemed to really help, in that he understood the baby had different needs than him, but that he was still valued, even if we couldn't drop everything that second.

The doctor told us that the number one thing to watch out for when bringing a sibling home, is their safety. This really surprised me, but she warned us that while the kids don't have malicious intent, their wanting to help can actually make things worse. She told us a story of when she was a baby, and her brother, who was younger than five at the time, picked her up because she was crying and tried to take her upstairs to her mom. He ended up dropping her and she had to get stitches as a baby. This shocked me that kids would think like this, but it makes sense. Very quickly, safety became our priority.

For the first few months, we started having visitors at different times and it was nice, especially if they came over to play with my son and not just be with the baby. We were in a good place as a family together, we felt God's presence in our lives daily, my anxiety was a lot lower, and my husband took off work like he did for the first to stay home, which helped so much. We were very fortunate to have this time together.

Some things to keep in mind after you have a baby are that you should start planning for the future. After having a baby, you get a tax deduction which in 2022 was

$2,000 per child up to age sixteen. You should also put together a Will to determine who watches your kids if you both die, who takes over the house and finances, what you are leaving the kids, etc.

You can also set up a 529 Education Plan that is a state sponsored investment plan that you can save money for your kids and build the funds with the market. Then you can withdraw funds tax-free to cover almost any type of college expense when they are ready.

Another option is to set up an Indexed Universal Life Insurance policy for you and your kids. It lasts the entire life and builds on cash value through their life along with a death benefit. You can pull funds whenever you'd like and there are no penalties.

If you are able, these are some of the things you can do to ensure your kids are set up for success in the future even if it's just saving a little at a time.

After planning and thinking we had it all figured out, the most unexpected, extraordinary thing happened, something that we could never have imagined.
Coronavirus.

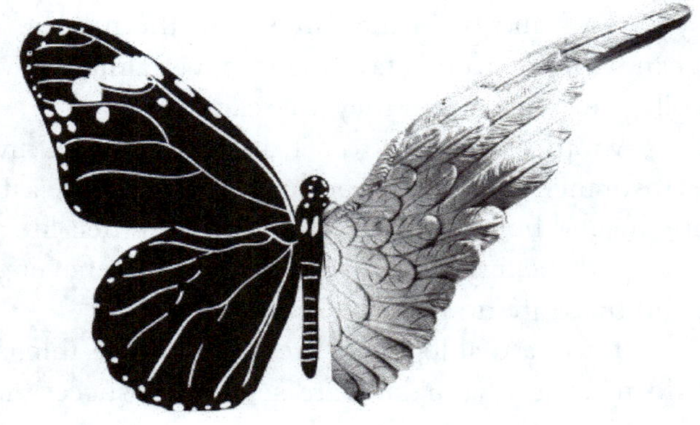

"You **must** do the thing
you think you cannot do."
Eleanor Roosevelt

CHAPTER 16

Chaos When the World Was Forced to Rest

OUR CUTE LITTLE EXHAUSTED FAMILY OF FOUR NOW. AS ALWAYS, PUMPING WHILE EVERYONE TOOK BABY WATCH DUTY.

I was starting to get excited to go back to work and get a break from taking care of two kids 24/7. Don't get me wrong, having three months off for maternity leave is great, but it is *not* a vacation. I was beginning to get cabin fever again and needed something more in my life so I could feel like I was a productive human being to society.

I am fortunate to work for an extraordinary company and manager so I called my manager and asked if I could work from home on the days my husband works, so that I could avoid daycare, and thankfully, he said yes. I began to get ready for my return to work, packing up all my office items, planning the breakfast and lunch ideas I could take to work. Not to mention, the idea of being around people—specifically grown-ups with which I could have a real conversation not about my kids—exhilarated me.

But the closer my return date came, the closer this invisible thing was slowly spreading our way and we didn't know it would change our entire world.

Before we knew it, the entire United States was shut down because of Covid.

When I had my second child, I had had a plan and it had been derailed. I was excited to go back to work. I would be able to get a break from the kids. I would be better able to handle my postpartum feelings. As they say, if you want to make God laugh, tell Him your plans.

The first few weeks were okay because it was a challenge. I like a challenge. I'm Type-A remember? Could I work from home and be a mom, sure, why not? My son was still able to attend daycare for a while because my husband is a firefighter and they stayed open to first responders. So, I'd put my daughter in her swing, walker, or highchair during my meetings and get my work done. This worked out really well for a while. I even thought, hey, maybe there will be some perks to this Covid thing. I could breastfeed or pump from home without worrying about who'd see me or comment about it. I could cuddle with my daughter way more than I would've if I'd gone to work. I could easily take a break and go on a walk around the park. I had an easier time starting work without having to rush around in the morning trying to get to the office on time.

But as the weeks turned into months; it got very real and very lonely very quick. It was fine, at first, to keep everyone at a distance because we didn't want to get anyone sick, especially with my husband being a first responder. Neither did we want others to get the baby sick, since we knew very little about the disease. We figured, as long as we were home together, everything was fine. But this meant if we were home together, everyone was kept away, and we had to isolate ourselves even further from any help or support we may have gotten.

I remember the moment we found out someone we knew was sick, and how scary it became. I remember I had to literally stop watching the news because every single news cycle they'd report the numbers for our city and county. As the count for Covid began to rise rapidly, so did my anxiety. I was so concerned about the kids getting sick, I was already trying to protect them from everything and now I had to keep them in an invisible bubble because I thought they were going to die from the virus. I knew our family wanted to support us by coming over to help, but we were too nervous about getting anyone sick. It felt as though there was this invisible thing controlling my life.

I chose to make people wear masks, even if they were ten feet away—and I know I wasn't the only one to do that. I would disinfect everything in sight, including the groceries, deliveries, or mail.

I mentioned the passing of my grandmother and unfortunately the last two years of her life took place in this Covid season. My heart breaks at the thought that she had to spend most of it alone. Nobody wanted to get her sick, so we'd try to do drive-by visits if we were in the area, to just say hello. We'd buy breakfast and eat outside together so she could see the kids. My son even made her a gift that was his two handprints connected by a string the length of his arms, which was supposed to be a life size hug from him.

I treasure these memories because, even though we didn't get to see her often, we made every effort to make her happy and comfortable during this time and we saw her as much as we could. We tried to make sure she knew she was seen and loved.

Months turned into a year, and my kids celebrated their birthdays in the pandemic. It was a struggle to decide what to do. Of course, we didn't want anyone to get sick, so we ended up having a drive-by party for my son and only having our immediate family come over at separate times (while also wearing masks) to celebrate my daughter's birthday. It was hard because how do you explain to your kids they can't have a party, without freaking them out? How do you explain to your kids that everyone has to wear a mask. This was not normal for my son but it became my daughter's normal. We did our best and they understood as best they could. All they cared about was the cake and presents anyway.

I always had this cool little idea in the back of my mind, that we would raise our kids the same, with all the same experiences. That way they would be equal, and life would be fair to them.

When Covid hit, there was literally no way I could do that. Everything was different between how My son grew up and how my daughter grew up. It's not how we planned it, but they are unique in their own ways. To try to put things into perspective a little, my little girl literally didn't have a chance to learn people's faces until after she was around a year old. It took her a while to adjust to match people's voices to their faces.

Looking back, I'm not entirely sure how we made it through. We would take the kids outside as much as we could so they wouldn't feel cooped up. We would take turns having a shift with the kids so the other could rest, sleep, or be alone for a second. Like any new mom should, we prioritized being with our kids over having a clean house, clean clothes, or a clean sink. I don't know how many different art projects we did. We read so many books. We also watched a whole lot of T.V., especially when I had to work, and my husband was at work.

As parents, we did what we had to do. Any help that we may have had was now obsolete. The friendships and socialization we had were gone. All of our friends had to continue working, so it's not like we could just call them and chit-chat all day. It was literally us and the kids, and that was it. The face-to-face contact with people was ten feet away. The breaks from the kids we used to have were—wait, *what* breaks? (Being a parent, you literally have no breaks. Even after we would put the kids to sleep for a nap or bedtime, my body was constantly on edge thinking they were going to wake up screaming, fall out of bed, cry, have a bad dream, and any chance of peace I thought I had, would be gone in a blink of an eye). Even to this day three years later, I still feel this anxiety.

This is where I had to double down on the coping mechanisms I had learned in the past few years. I knew my body would get out-of-whack if I went too long without doing yoga. I was using the Calm app to meditate before bed because I knew getting a good night's sleep was extremely important for anxiety and depression. My husband would let me sleep as much as I needed to during the day, and I mean literally 12 hours if I needed to and would do his best at keeping the kids quiet. I would go for small little walks or runs to clear my mind, get outside, and try to pretend just for a second that I didn't have the pressure and responsibility of the world on my shoulders to raise two good humans. I would shower. I know this seems miniscule but after getting in the shower, washing my hair, and shaving my legs, I was a new woman. Like Shania Twain says, "Man, I feel like a woman." Who knew that a clean body can also feel like a clean slate for your mind.

Having more than one kid has its own challenges, but the thought of my son not having a sibling, far outweighed any pain or suffering I was going to have to endure to have a second baby. I grew up with a brother who is twelve years older than me which at times was great but he seemed more like a father to me than a brother. I wanted my son to have memories with a sibling close in age where they could, play at the park, make up imaginary friends, have sleep overs, play sports, ride to school, be able to learn from each other and grow up together. They would always have a built-in best friend that they could lean on for anything and always trust.

" We do not have the
power to demand who our
children will be;
however,
we can be instruments in
the hands of our
Redeemer in shaping who
our children
are becoming
day by day."
~Unknown

CHAPTER 17

Give God Your Weakness and He'll Give You His Strength

OUR FIRST OFFICIAL FAMILY PHOTO

No matter how hard Covid was, I know we went through it for a reason. I think, for a lot of us, it puts things into perspective. All the things we thought were important, were suddenly not. All the things God wants us to focus on, became brighter. We were literally forced to stop living for society and start living together as a family for God.

Having two kids definitely changed our life. If you asked me today if I would do it all over, I would still say, 100%, yes. But the only caveat I'd tell you, is to wait to have kids. I'd tell you to do everything you want to do, including what's on your bucket list and don't wait! Get to know yourself a little bit more so that you are not trying to find yourself in the middle of having babies. Because as I've learned, the worry and anxiety never go away. It will increase when you get pregnant and even more after you have kids.

The first question my therapist asked me was, "Why are you here?" I told her I wasn't sure, but I needed my anxiety to stop. She kindly told me that that would never happen, but with the tools she was going to teach me, I'd be able to learn to manage it, rather than let it consume me.

They say once you get through a milestone with your child, the worry never stops, it just changes. This is so true. Just when we thought we had conquered breast-feeding, we'd need to start solid foods. Just when we thought we'd conquered crawling, they start walking. Just when we thought we'd conquered sleeping, they go through a sleep regression. Just when we thought we had two tiny babies, we blinked and had a six and a three-year-old.

Two very unique six and three-year-olds. Because of their experiences, they are both very different kids. My son is very shy, calm, and such an empathetic child. My daughter is very loud, brave, and outgoing. They balance each other out and they have so much love for each other. I literally have to pull them off each other at night because they don't want to let go while saying good night. We have tried to instill in them the importance of family. Having a sibling is extremely important because they are the only family members that will be with you most of your life. Your parents will leave you eventually, and your spouse comes to you later in life, but you will have your sibling with you almost your entire life, if you are lucky. It had been important to us to have two kids around the same age.

Because we had a miscarriage their age difference was a little wider than we wanted, but it turned out perfect. Looking back now at the little girl who was so overwhelmed she didn't want to have anything to do with her kids after birth, I feel like a completely different person. Through my faith, I was able to give my life up to God and he showed me the only way through is through him. I have such a fierce love for my kids that I want to protect them from all life's evils. I want to make sure they know that they are destined for so much more than they know. I want to ensure they have the tools as children that I never did to get through anything. I want them to know that God is with them through anything even when it doesn't feel like it. I now know what that feeling of unconditional love is and don't ever take one minute for granted on how I am helping shape their futures. I love them so much it hurts my heart sometimes.

It is unimaginable, now writing this book, to think about all the things we went through to get where we are. Society's unfair expectations on parents is never-ending: stay hydrated, do laundry, do the dishes, clean the house, exercise, take care of the kids, eat healthy, rest often, work hard, go back to work, wait no, stay home with kids, be a good wife, keep up with your friends, visit your family, oh and don't forget to breast feed, take a shower, put on make-up, have sex, and put a smile on your face.

Just breathe and you'll be okay. But nothing is ever really "okay." We do the best with what we have. But the trenches of motherhood are just hard. They're simply survival sometimes. I saw once that after flamingos have babies, they feed them their milk and because it's so draining, they are literally drained of their pink color. They actually turn white the entire time they feed their kids and their color comes back eventually after the kids start eating on their own.

Did my husband and I go to couples therapy during this time?

We sure did.

Did I get into big arguments with my parents about the decisions we were making for our kids?

I sure did.

Did I sometimes need to go on a run to get away from everything and take a break?

I sure did.

Did I still cry in times of depression or anxiety?

I sure did.

Do I still have moments of overwhelming suffocation?

Yes, I do.

Did we have to navigate the death of someone close?

We did, together.

Did I ever think motherhood was going to be this hard?

No, I sure didn't.

Did I ever realize motherhood would be so rewarding?

No, I sure didn't.

I knew something was missing even after having two kids. I knew that all this knowledge and experience that I went through and gained was not just happenstance but was for a larger purpose. Interacting with so many kinds of mothers throughout my life, I never would've imagined motherhood being this exhausting, both physically and mentally. I was getting more and more frustrated with each step of motherhood, that nobody warned me of the big things. It's nobody's fault, there just is a total lack of awareness of the journey of motherhood.

So, once again, that's why I wrote this book.

I hope that it was informative.

Know that you are appreciated.

You are changing the trajectory of the world by raising good humans.

I hope that you realize, being a parent, you are not alone.

I hope that in supporting new parents, you realize how impactful your support is.

You may be a mother, but you are more than a mother.

I challenge you to do the hard things, to find joy in God, and to enjoy the little things.

These moments of heartache and hardship are just momentary. You are not the first person to go through these things, you are not alone going through these things, and you will not be the last. With each day, things do get better. Things do get a little easier.

I don't know if I've ever prayed so much before being a mother. Before, all my prayers were very selfish. Now my prayers are mainly to thank God for everything he's given me and including all of the uncomfortable experiences and keep my family healthy and safe. Everything else comes after.

I promise, just like the flamingo mamas, you will find your pink again.

"She was becoming **HERSELF** casting aside that fictitious self which we assume like a garment."
~Kate Chopin~

Afterward

This overwhelming experience is one I will never forget because I know God put me through it for a reason. As Glennon Doyle says, "We can do hard things," and I hope my journey helps and  inspires others. I hope my kids see me as an example that they can do anything they put their minds to. I hope they know that they are not defined by labels of who people think they are but by who they choose to become.

Without my faith helping me through this time in my life, I don't know what would've happened, or where I would be. Even though I had doubts at times, I knew God was always with me and I am living my life for Him. Everything I do matters, and I feel as though the specific things I've gone through are to be able to help others who are planning to have a child (parent or not). I want to support those who will be or are going through the same trauma.

I am so inspired by those parents who do it all alone or with little support. I have a huge family and friends support system that I know God has put in my life for a reason. My mom taught me a lot about being a mother from just being there for me. Although I may not remember a lot of my childhood, I always knew my mom was there to listen, to support, to cheer on, to love me, to hug me, to inspire me. I want to thank my mom for unequivocally loving me no matter what and teaching me what it means to not only be a mother but be a "Mom."

God gave me two grandmothers, even for just a short time. My daughter's middle name is Marlo after my grandmother's child, who she lost very quickly soon after giving birth. The day that Marlo passed away was the same date that my husband was born, although it be decades later. This is a God wink if you ask me. I want to thank my two grandmas who molded me into the woman I am today, and I cannot wait to see you again.

I thank my aunties and uncles for always being like a set of fairy godmothers and godfathers to me. My dad, for always having my back and teaching me one of life's greatest lessons, that life isn't fair and to kick ass and take names. My brother and sister in law, for being my second set of parents at times when I needed it. To my brother and sister in law, thank you for accepting me into your family and letting me be a part of your life. My husband's parents for raising the man of my dreams. You all are appreciated more than you know.

For those husbands and partners who do it all, I praise you. My husband is truly my other half. From the moment I met him when I was fifteen, he knew me better than I knew myself. He has always pushed me to feel more like myself. He challenges me to be better, think differently, and love wholeheartedly. At this point in my life, I've known my husband longer than I haven't known him and that is something weird to think about! I never would've imagined God would bless us with such a beautiful loving family. My husband has given me everything I've ever wanted and then some. Even throughout this difficult time in our lives, we found joy. We knew we would always be there for each other and get through anything together. I love you so much and appreciate you more than I could ever explain or be able to even put in words. Thank you for everything you do for our family.

ALL my past and current friends. Each of you was put into my life for a specific reason and I cherish every second we spent or spend together. I could lean on you to help me through hard times and celebrate with me through the good times. Having someone to listen, cry, travel, laugh, love, and do life together is such an exhilarating comforting feeling. I appreciate each of you for being there for me in different times of my life for different reasons. I love you and thank you for showing up.

My editor Samantha Rae Ortiz, who I am honored to be a sister in Christ with through our college-days in a Christian Sorority, Sigma Alpha Omega. I had no idea where to even start with editing this book, but you supported me and ensured my book was important and impactful in honoring mothers and parents for who they are, and reminding everyone there is hope.

I celebrate all parents, single parents, single moms, moms of multiples, moms who have lost, moms who passed on too soon, stay at home moms, working moms, mom's who may not be ready to be moms, all women. You are the true superheroes of this world. You should be celebrated every damn day. It's so mysterious to me thinking through who your kids will turn out to be. As babies they are so little and innocent and as they grow into themselves, you begin to see their image, their facial features, their personalities, and their love.

I'll end with a quote from the character Lucas Scott on my favorite show *One Tree Hill*, "Most of our lives are a series of images, they pass us by like towns on a highway. But sometimes a moment stuns us as it happens and we know that this instant is more than a fleeting image. We know that this moment, every part of it will live on forever."

To my kids,

You have come into my life by God's grace and changed it for the better. I may not always be patient, calm, or the best mother, but I am *your* mother. I love you so much my heart could burst. You have given me the strength I needed to find myself, be myself, and love myself. Don't ever forget our mantra: You are smart, you are brave, you are strong, and

You can do anything!

Dad and I may not always be here physically, but we hope the lessons we are teaching you now stick, and you find the confidence and bravery to do what you set out to do in this life with God at your side.

Remember that life is not fair, and you never get a second chance to make a first impression. People and friends will come and go in your life and that's ok. People are not immortal and can be gone in a second, so treat every time you see someone as if it was the last. Appreciate people often and let them know it. Love with all your heart even if it's scary and you end up getting hurt. The risk of love is loss but still take chances and say, I love you. Who you choose to spend your life with matters. Make sure you choose someone who makes you a better person when you are with them.

Experience things more than you collect things. Travel often. Dream big and don't ever let anyone tell you to think small. Life is not always butterflies and rainbows but trust in God and he will get you through anything. Stand up and let your voice be heard. Sometimes life throws you challenges but remember what small potatoes things can be. Tell the truth always, even if it's uncomfortable. Don't worry about what other people think and pay more attention to people's actions, not their words. Live your true life and be who you want to be and do what you want to do.

Lastly, whatever you choose to do, do it with all your heart. I love you forever.

Your mom,

Mariah

HERE'S TO STRONG

Women

MAY WE Know THEM

MAY WE Be THEM

MAY WE Raise THEM

All The Things